The Soviet Union: A Very Short Introduction

VERY SHORT INTRODUCTIONS are for anyone wanting a stimulating and accessible way into a new subject. They are written by experts, and have been translated into more than 45 different languages.

The series began in 1995, and now covers a wide variety of topics in every discipline. The VSI library now contains over 500 volumes—a Very Short Introduction to everything from Psychology and Philosophy of Science to American History and Relativity—and continues to grow in every subject area.

Titles in the series include the following:

Stephen Lovell

THE SOVIET UNION

A Very Short Introduction

OXFORD

UNIVERSITY PRESS

Great Clarendon Street, Oxford OX2 6DP

Oxford University Press is a department of the University of Oxford.
It furthers the University's objective of excellence in research, scholarship,
and education by publishing worldwide in

Oxford New York

Auckland Cape Town Dar es Salaam Hong Kong Karachi
Kuala Lumpur Madrid Melbourne Mexico City Nairobi
New Delhi Shanghai Taipei Toronto

With offices in

Argentina Austria Brazil Chile Czech Republic France Greece
Guatemala Hungary Italy Japan Poland Portugal Singapore
South Korea Switzerland Thailand Turkey Ukraine Vietnam

Oxford is a registered trade mark of Oxford University Press
in the UK and in certain other countries

Published in the United States
by Oxford University Press Inc., New York

British Library Cataloguing in Publication Data

Data available

Library of Congress Cataloging in Publication Data

Data available

Typeset by SPI Publisher Services, Pondicherry, India
Printed in Great Britain by
Ashford Colour Press Ltd., Gosport, Hampshire.

ISBN 978-0-19-923848-4

Contents

Acknowledgements

Work on this book was greatly eased by the award of a Philip Leverhulme Prize. I thank the Leverhulme Trust for its generous support.

I gratefully acknowledge the assistance of Luciana O'Flaherty, Andrea Keegan, and OUP's external readers as the book went from commission to completion. Many thanks also to the colleagues who kindly read parts or the whole of the manuscript: Catriona Kelly cast her keen eye over a full draft, while Jeremy Smith and Julian Graffy offered helpful comments on individual chapters.

My greatest debt is to the many scholars whose work I have used without having the opportunity for adequate acknowledgement. To them I offer grateful apologies.

List of illustrations

List of maps

Introduction: questions and approaches

In early November 1917, a revolutionary socialist party known as the Bolsheviks seized power in Petrograd amidst the ruins of a Russian empire that had come apart months earlier under the pressure of world war. In December 1922, having defeated its adversaries in an apocalyptic civil war, the revolutionary regime was able to announce the creation of a new state, the Union of Soviet Socialist Republics. At the end of the 1920s, proclaiming its goal of building a powerful modern state and economy, this USSR embarked on a programme of breakneck industrialization and forced collectivization of agriculture. Over the next 15 years, it imprisoned, exiled, or executed millions of people who were deemed to stand in its way: peasants, ethnic groups, intellectuals, 'marginals' (anything from market traders to down-and-outs), and political 'enemies' of other varieties. The Soviet state then withstood its greatest test when it came through a world war, losing in the process almost 27 million of its citizens. A few years later, in the mid-1950s, the regime of its own accord drastically reduced the violence on which it had hitherto relied so heavily. While the Soviet system became less inhumane, it proved unable to keep up the frenetic growth of the 1930s or to meet the challenges of social modernization and the post-industrial economy. In the mid-1980s, mindful of these problems, the leadership embarked on a programme of economic and political reform that soon weakened its control over society and its authority. In December 1991, unable to withstand the pace of events, the Soviet Union found itself signed out of existence.

Timeline of Soviet history

(Note: dates up to February 1918 were 13 days behind Western Europe.)

February–March 1917: popular unrest and army mutiny bring abdication of Emperor Nicholas II; power shared by Provisional Government and Petrograd Soviet of Workers and Soldiers' Deputies

October 1917: Bolshevik Party under Vladimir Lenin seizes power in Petrograd

Summer 1918: Civil War starts in earnest

1921: end of Civil War; Bolsheviks announce New Economic Policy; outbreak of famine on the Volga

December 1922: establishment of Union of Soviet Socialist Republics

January 1924: death of Lenin

1928: launch of first Five-Year Plan

1929: Joseph Stalin achieves domination of Bolshevik Party; start of forced collectivization of agriculture

1931–3: famine kills around six million people

1936–8: show trials of leading Bolsheviks; mass terror kills around 750,000

1939: Nazi–Soviet pact (August); Soviet forces invade Poland (September)

June 1941: Germany invades The Soviet Union

May 1945: capitulation of Nazi Germany

March 1953: death of Joseph Stalin

1954–5: Nikita Khrushchev emerges as Stalin's successor

February 1956: Khrushchev delivers 'Secret Speech' denouncing Stalin

1964: Khrushchev ousted and replaced by Leonid Brezhnev
December 1979: Soviet forces enter Afghanistan
1982: Brezhnev dies; is replaced by Yuri Andropov
1984: Andropov dies; is replaced by Konstantin Chernenko
1985: Chernenko dies; is replaced by Mikhail Gorbachev
1986: Gorbachev announces 'perestroika' reform programme
1989: partially contested elections to Congress of People's Deputies
1991: failure of coup by party, military, and security elite (August); collapse of The Soviet Union (December)

This stark chronological sketch brings to the fore two inescapable facts about the country that forms the subject of this book. First, for the first three decades of its existence, it was the scene of appalling violence and suffering. Second, its history has an obvious narrative shape: revolutionary upsurge, bloody rise of dictatorship, victory and partial vindication in World War II, followed by attenuated liberalization and slide into late industrial obsolescence.

These two points have almost overpowering implications for how one might decide to write a book about the USSR. The illiberal and oppressive character of Soviet rule, especially in the period 1917–53, has rightly driven many observers to ask who (or what) was responsible for the violence. And the (now completed) historical trajectory of the Soviet Union seems to follow a bell curve of steep rise, precarious stability, and precipitous fall.

This book, however, will take a rather different path. Its chapters will be defined thematically rather than chronologically, an approach that seems to me to be preferable on general principles for a book as short as this: a straightforward linear account would have to be sketchy to the point of self-parody. The 'decline and fall' story has been told about the Soviet Union so many times already that there seems little point in rehearsing it further. My primary analytical aim in this book will be not to show when and how the USSR went wrong, or to speculate on when exactly its collapse became inevitable, but rather to explain the workings of a society, economy, and political system very alien to Britons or Americans in the early 21st century. I want to characterize the Soviet Union, not to pronounce sentence on it.

In the process, I would like to try to show what a remarkable creation this country was: remarkable in the sense that it held together for so long despite so many sources of external threat and internal unease. No doubt all societies and political systems contain contradictions and tensions, but in the Soviet Union they were exceptionally acute. In order to bring them out, each chapter shows the interaction through time of a pair of contrasting principles. I start, in Chapter 1, with the Soviet Union's own sense of its historical trajectory: how did its uniquely forward-looking ideology come to make sense of the Soviet past? Chapter 2 moves from the realm of ideas and imagination to matters of implementation and political practice: it shows how the notorious terrorist proclivities of the Soviet state were modulated by an ideology of grass-roots social mobilization and collectivism. The next two chapters draw attention to economic and social dimensions of the Soviet experience: they show how a purportedly egalitarian society found room for hierarchy and inequality, how an authoritarian regime attempted to be of the people as well as in the people's name, and how the peasants, workers, and soldiers of 1917 became a very different kind of 'mass' society over the decades of Soviet power. The final pair of chapters places the Soviet Union in multinational and international contexts. Chapter 5 analyses Soviet efforts to combine one strong state with a multiplicity of ethnic and linguistic groups, while Chapter 6 surveys the ambivalent Soviet relationship – both geopolitical and cultural – with the wider world. My aim throughout the book is to defamiliarize my object of inquiry – perhaps the most widely and

4

polemically discussed country in modern history – without making it unrecognizable.

That is not to say that familiar accounts are uncontentious. If we measure our Soviet history in terms of the tenure of leaders, the story is straightforward: revolutionary Lenin begets tyrannical Stalin, who is succeeded (and then denounced) by the wayward Khrushchev, whose eccentricities are terminated by the stolid but increasingly invalid Brezhnev, who expires to make way for two more sickly leaders, Andropov and Chernenko, before the energetic new broom of Mikhail Gorbachev brings the house down. But if we are interested not just in political succession but in the waxing and waning of the Soviet 'system', or of a Soviet 'order', or even of a Soviet 'civilization', things are far less clear.

In formal terms, the USSR was created in 1922. At that moment most of its defining features were already in place. Power was held by a Bolshevik Party that stood behind the Soviet state and was itself buttressed by a radical version of Marxism. A political police existed on a stable footing and had extensive powers. The revolutionary regime was committed to ruling over a large multinational state. Russia was on its way to becoming a recognized European power once more, having survived the seven-year turmoil from the start of World War I to the end of the Civil War.

But it is possible to compile an equally impressive list of ways in which the USSR was *not* yet what we might think of as quintessentially Soviet. There was little sense of how a regime based in Moscow might rule over an enormous, widely dispersed, multi-ethnic population. Although the Bolsheviks were ferociously antipathetic to 'bourgeois' commerce, they had just retreated, with the institution of the New Economic Policy, from the requisitioning and centralizing economic policies of the Civil War. The defining economic features of the Soviet system – central planning, overwhelming emphasis on heavy industry – were yet to appear. It was still unclear how the ruling party would in non-emergency conditions relate to the state and to society. And so on.

The number of unresolved issues that we find in 1922 has led many historians to ask the basic question: when did the Revolution end, and when did a stable 'Sovietness' take hold? Over the past few decades the dates of the Russian Revolution have become highly variable. Orlando Figes, in his acclaimed *A People's Tragedy*, chooses 1891–1924. The Harvard doyen Richard Pipes starts in 1899 and stops in 1924. Sheila Fitzpatrick, after briefly sketching the historical backdrop, plunges her readers into the thick of events in 1917 and takes her story to 1932. S. A. Smith, my distinguished predecessor in the Very Short Introduction series, adopts a similar solution to the problem of periodization, ending his account in the late 1920s. Peter Holquist sees the Revolution and the onset of Bolshevik dictatorship as the outcome of a 'continuum of crisis' initiated by the entry of tsarist Russia into World War I in August 1914. Only one generalization is more or less safe: to write a history of the Russian Revolution that focuses exclusively on the year 1917 is nowadays desperately unfashionable.

The choice of dates, of course, is far from value-neutral. Figes, in his quest for the broad social and political canvas and the view 'from below', opens with the famine of 1891–2. Pipes, who sees the Revolution largely as the result of left-wing revolutionary conspiracy and ideological malevolence, takes student unrest in 1899 as his point of departure. Fitzpatrick and Smith – both social historians, one known for her work on social mobility, the other for studies of worker politics and culture – start with the upheaval of 1917 and follow it through to crash industrialization and collectivization. Nor, in principle, is there any reason why a historian of revolutionary Russia should feel obliged to stop in the early 1930s: such was the level of social and political conflict in the USSR that one might perfectly well choose to think of a 'Soviet Civil War' running from 1918 to 1953 (with perhaps a brief ceasefire in the 1920s, when everyone gathered their breath and regrouped).

As well as being intellectually consequential, such matters of periodization are morally fraught. Since there are few people (outside Russia, at least) who regard collectivization, Stalinist dictatorship, and the Great Terror as good things, the key question is when the rot set in. When did violent dictatorship become a medium-term certainty rather than a short-term expedient? Whom or what should we hold responsible for this: Lenin, Stalin, the Bolshevik Party, the brutality of the Civil War, Bolshevik ideology, the socially disintegrative effects of headlong urbanization and industrialization?

Even if we can for a moment agree on when the Sovietness of the USSR took its final shape, that still leaves open the question of what exactly this unlovely abstraction entailed. How 'modern' was the Soviet Union, and how 'traditional'? How can we best characterize the story of this country – as progress (however brutally achieved), as a botched or aberrant version of industrial modernity, as the latest chapter in the long history of Russian despotism?

And finally, now that we have an end-point for Soviet history that is less contentious than its start date, what conclusions should we draw from the fact of the collapse of the USSR? When did the decline of Soviet socialism begin? Was the Soviet system unreformable?

The questions listed in the previous three paragraphs have been endlessly debated. A few answers to them may emerge from the chapters that follow in this book. But for the time being it is worth reflecting on what basis we might try to answer them.

What historians choose to argue is usually inseparable from how they get hold of, and select, their material. In this sense, the Soviet

Union has since 1991 become a moving target for historical enquiry: although the country has been erased from the map, the sources available to study it have increased exponentially. For almost the whole of the Soviet period, historians within the USSR were severely constrained in what they could say about their own history, while non-Soviet commentators were severely constrained in what they could find out about the main questions that interested them: the inner workings of the one-party state, the mechanisms of state terror, the extent of popular support for the regime and of resistance to it. Soviet published records (books, journals, newspapers, broadcasts) contained strategic distortions and silences, while archival holdings on most subjects were off-limits. Admittedly, postwar researchers had a few windfalls. A substantial chunk of the archive of the Soviet party organization in Smolensk, a large province in the west of the Soviet Union, was seized by the invading Germans in 1941 and later came into the hands of the Americans: this 'Smolensk archive' would inspire some pioneering Western accounts of the pre-war Soviet system. A few years later, a group of researchers at Harvard University, funded by the US Air Force, tracked down close to 3,000 displaced former Soviet citizens, seeing their unique potential as informants on the Soviet Union from within. In 1950–1, mainly in West Germany, 764 in-depth interviews were conducted for this Harvard Project on the Soviet Social System. The resulting 61 bound volumes of transcripts formed the basis for a key set of highly influential studies.

Between the 1950s and the mid-1980s, many fine studies of Soviet history were written, but there remained a nagging suspicion that Western scholars might be inferring too much from too little, while the only Russians who were able to comment freely on their own history were émigrés. Then, in the Gorbachev era, most historical taboos were lifted, and by the early 1990s Russian archives were opening their doors to Western researchers and – even more remarkably – delivering many of the documents that those researchers wanted to see. Soviet history had suddenly become a very different kind of pursuit, and this archival boom promised great insights.

But exactly what kind of insights? Some people expected the archives to adjudicate in a scholarly dispute that had for some time taken over the field of Soviet history (partly to its intellectual detriment). This debate pitted the adherents of a 'totalitarian' theory (according to which state dominated society by means of a single ideology and instruments of control such as the political police, and the Bolshevik leadership was unequivocally responsible for the appalling violence of the first half of the Soviet period) against 'revisionists' (who tended to look for the social origins and contexts of events).

As is usually the case in scholarly debate, both sides could claim vindication in the new sources. Believers in the strong, 'totalitarian' state found conclusive evidence of the culpability of Soviet leaders – in the first instance Stalin – for wrecking the lives of millions of people. Numerous smoking guns were discovered lying around in the archives of this secretive but profusely documented state (even if the most sensitive materials, which no doubt contain a whole arsenal, remain off-limits in a 'Presidential' archive). The archives have also shed light on many matters of moral as well as historiographical import: the numbers and categories of victims of terror, the conduct of mass resettlement programmes, the scale and nature of uprisings against the authorities.

The social historians, for their part, could claim that the state whose workings were exposed to scrutiny in these archival documents was anything but the smooth centralized operation that the totalitarian theory might imply. It was staffed by harried, overworked, inadequately trained, self-interested, corrupt, or plain incompetent officials. Its leadership was often poorly informed on key policy matters, and its control of some regions and groups was at best precarious. From this perspective, the analytical bottom line of the new archival research was more or less: 'things were a lot more complicated and chaotic than one might think'. The archives added texture without necessarily changing any paradigms.

But paradigms *were* changing, for reasons that were not entirely to do with the archives. The political passions of the Cold War were starting to die down. It was possible to adjust downwards the figures for executions during the Great Terror, or to argue that Stalin was not directly responsible for all of these killings, without drawing the charge of communist sympathies. Even among the most devout fellow travellers, there were probably not too many people who believed that the Soviet Union in the 1930s was an easy or a pleasant place to be, and there were even fewer such people in the postcommunist era. To arraign the Soviet experience was no longer necessary. It was hardly in doubt (if it ever had been) that the Soviet Union for at least half its existence was poor and brutal, and that tens of millions of Soviet people suffered in ways that, in the early 21st century, even Russians (let alone Americans or Britons) will find hard to imagine. But the search for culprits, or the drawing of conclusions about the viability of the Soviet order, no longer seemed such urgent tasks. The key questions now were not 'Who was responsible?' or 'How long will it last?' but rather 'How was it possible?' and even 'What was it [the Soviet Union] like?' Increasingly sceptical about the rationality and efficiency of the Soviet state, historians were switching their attention from political control to the unintended consequences of that control. Now that our chronological perspective is lengthening, and the less violent postwar decades seem as worthy of historical investigation as the bloody and turbulent pre-war era that used to define Soviet history as a field, it is less rewarding to assess the Soviet Union merely as a form of dictatorship. The USSR not only killed and oppressed people, it also educated them, gave them jobs, and (more sinisterly) handed them opportunities to abuse and manipulate their fellow citizens. The notion of dictatorship tends to obscure the diversity of attitudes that Soviet people might take to their regime: these ranged from hatred and fear to passionate devotion, with opportunism, pragmatism, loyalty, and entitlement somewhere in between.

Letter from a female blood donor to the Central Committee of the Communist Party, 29 March 1943

When you hear on the radio about the government's concern for our people, you can't help thinking, why is there no concern for donors who give their blood to save the lives of our soldiers. I am a senior donor from even before the war. I'm in the first category. I'm a home guardist. That means I don't get money for giving blood [...] But in shops I have to queue for 3–4 hours to get my [special donor's] 'ration'. I don't get the whole ration on a single day, but at various times, and half of it is poor quality or adulterated. [...]

Society sees us as 'lucky ones' (we have a worker's ration card) and doesn't want to help us. For example, on the days people give blood not all institutions let donors off work. Or we get thrown at us comments like 'I don't think you're doing it out of a sense of patriotism but just for the benefits'. I suggested to this non-politically-conscious comrade that he could become a donor, but he replied: 'My health is more important to me than that ration'.

At one level, this woman's decision to give blood is likely to be pragmatic and self-interested: the extra rations might well make the difference between life and death in conditions of wartime scarcity. But also significant are the identity and sense of purpose she derives from this activity. She presents herself both as a good patriot and as the voice of an important social constituency in the war effort: for her, as for many other Soviet people, words like 'donor' and 'home guardist' were not just occupations but badges of honour. This sense of self-worth gives her strong feelings of entitlement: like millions of her fellow citizens during the Soviet period, she addresses a personal grievance to one of the highest political bodies in the Soviet Union. And her letter had an impact: the Central Committee passed it on to the People's Commissariat of Trade, which after an investigation concluded that the allegations of mistreatment of blood donors were largely true. This authoritarian state could at times be highly responsive to voices 'from below' – and, importantly, not only to denunciations.

In this light, the designation of the USSR as 'totalitarian' is not so much wrong as incomplete and intellectually limiting. It implies comparison with other regimes (Fascist Italy, Nazi Germany, Communist China) that may differ from the Soviet Union in many important respects. It is contaminated by the political rhetoric of the Cold War, which at times turned the concept of totalitarianism into a term of condemnation rather than a tool of analysis. Most of all, it does a bad job of explaining change over time. For the first half of its existence, the Soviet regime used terror as a first-resort technique of government; in the second half, it did not. Many people would agree that the USSR was totalitarian in 1937; rather fewer would attach this label to the country in 1985. When, in that case, did the Soviet Union cease to be totalitarian? Is it possible to be less than totally totalitarian? How many key attributes of the phenomenon can be subtracted before it starts to lose its shape?

To ask such questions is not to deny the undeniable. No amount of revisionism is likely to shake the conventional wisdom that the Bolsheviks were devoted to the exercise of power through a disciplined and centralized party-state. Their foremost revolutionary tactician and ideological founding father, Vladimir Lenin, deserves a place in the history of political thought not for his

Marxist analyses of class antagonism, or for his occasional utopian reflections on the future socialist society, but rather for his steely concentration on political realities. His bottom-line question was 'Who comes out on top?' (*Kto kogo?*, literally 'Who whom?'), and no amount of elaborate analysis of productive forces was going to distract him from it. Lenin ceased to play a leading part in events when he suffered a series of strokes in 1922–3, but his successors retained his commitment to defending Bolshevik power at all costs. To this end, they exiled or murdered political opponents, took measures against other groups of people who might constitute a threat, drove underground or abroad dissent within their own party, and ensured that people likely to be useful to them were better fed and housed than the average. They also proved expert in the black arts of propaganda and censorship. Library collections were purged, a new authoritative version of the Revolution took shape, and by the early 1930s Soviet newspapers, books, and films were fully employed producing convenient myths about socialist life.

Yet, although the commitment to centralized power was unambiguous, its consequences were not. Lenin's *Kto kogo?* was a great asset in a revolution, but it was a poor guide to running a complex modern state. Marxist-Leninist ideology presented itself as a 'scientific' world-view based on close and objective analysis of economic data, but it was usually bad at finding clear-cut solutions to practical problems. The language and the practice of politics in the Soviet Union were not as sharply defined as its leaders' sense of ideological certainty would imply. Labels like 'leftist', 'rightist', 'bourgeois', and 'deviationist' were regularly thrown at people in the 1920s and 1930s, and very often they stuck, but what these terms meant was unclear. For an ideology purportedly based on the values of Enlightenment rationalism, Soviet socialism made surprisingly extensive use of irrational sources of authority: leader cults, quasi-religious rituals, oracular pronouncements, public confession and recantation. In the interwar period, it resembled the Taliban or the Inquisition more than non-authoritarian socialist counterparts.

One does not have to try too hard to see further paradoxes of Soviet rule. This was a regime with an ideology of egalitarianism and social justice that was at the same time discriminatory from the very start. It oversaw a 'planned' and supposedly rational economy that led to chaos in resource distribution, *ad hoc* bargaining, and the creation of a dense network of patron–client relations. It headed a purportedly internationalist polity that turned inwards for much of its existence, most of the time adopting an anti-Western ideology that measured its success largely in terms defined by the West. And it operated in a patriarchal society, a land that the postwar sexual revolution never quite reached, yet one that enjoyed the highest rate of female labour force participation in the developed world and that claimed to have revolutionized gender relations.

The tendency, when discussing these paradoxes, has been to decry them as evidence of the Soviet regime's duplicity or to mourn them as the costs of attempting to implement a utopian ideology in a real, and highly imperfect, society. But these paradoxes are not impediments to a true understanding of the Soviet Union; to recognize them, as this book will attempt to show, is a first step towards that understanding.

Chapter 1
Future and past

Most governments have to perform a balancing act between the exigencies of the present and the prospects for the future. If in doubt – on issues such as pensions and the environment – they normally favour the present. The leaders of the Bolshevik state, by contrast, subordinated the present to the future. Soviet people were told insistently that they would work hard and live badly for a long and indefinite period of time – all this in the interests of building an abstract noun. In the words of the wry émigré commentators Pyotr Vail and Aleksandr Genis, Soviet ideology offered the following message: 'Life is wonderful! And it is wonderful above all because it will be even wonderfuller.' The Soviet Union was a state built on the myth of inexorable historical progress from darkness to light, from nationalism to internationalism, from poverty to prosperity, from class division to social unity.

Looking forward

This future orientation was not just a matter of political rhetoric. It was a way of thinking that permeated all public culture. As the statutes of the Soviet Writers' Union put it in 1934: 'Socialist realism, the basic method of Soviet literature and literary criticism, demands of the sincere writer a historically concrete presentation of reality in its revolutionary development.' Unvarnished depiction of life as it happened to be at any particular moment was false, since it did not take into account historical movement. It was like depicting a tennis ball without reference to its trajectory.

The Revolution, by contrast, had been presentist: in 1917, the Bolsheviks were able to proclaim instant benefits to society – land to the peasants, bread to the workers, peace to the soldiers. Yet, almost immediately, they began to undermine these benefits: they requisitioned grain from the peasantry, they imposed military discipline on the workers, and having extricated Russia from a world war they plunged it into a civil war.

The Bolsheviks could find justification for these measures not only in short-term imperatives but also in long-term objectives. In their reading of history, capitalism was bound in the long term to make way for communism. Capitalism carried within it the seeds of its own destruction. Based on the principle of anarchic economic competition, it would bring conflict and crisis as different groups fought over control of markets. It also led inevitably to greater social inequality, as an ever smaller group of bourgeois proprietors exploited the labouring population. According to Marxist revolutionary thinkers, these processes of capitalist disintegration accelerated in the early 20th century, as global capital took more monopolistic forms and bourgeois states entered a phase of mutually destructive economic rivalry. World War I would be thought of in Soviet Russia as the Imperialist War.

Capitalism, then, was doomed. But what was to replace it? What exactly was a revolution going to achieve? The orthodox view among Russian Marxists had long been that Russia would need not one revolution but two. The first, 'bourgeois', revolution would overthrow the tsarist order and put in place a liberal parliamentary regime. This interlude would give agrarian Russia the opportunity to increase its economic development – above all, to acquire a larger industrial working class – but it would not remove the social and economic tensions of capitalism. Rather, it would make the working class more conscious of these tensions and better able to take organized measures against them. In due course, when Russia was historically ready, it would have a 'proletarian' revolution.

The February Revolution of 1917 seemed to fit the description of a bourgeois revolution: it brought down the tsarist regime and installed a 'provisional government' dominated by liberal politicians. By other criteria, however, the diagnosis was not so neat: the provisional government had less control over the streets than workers' and soldiers' 'councils' (soviets) that were dominated by socialist parties, peasants were seizing land without asking anyone's permission, and Russia was still mired in an exhausting world war. Bourgeois consolidation and economic development were remote prospects in 1917.

This was the context in which the Bolshevik leader Vladimir Lenin returned to an idea he had advanced, with dismal results, during the defeated revolution of 1905. According to Lenin, Russia should not allow the bourgeoisie any piece of its revolution: the proletariat should take over immediately. Given that Russia was several historical steps short of the level of economic development that orthodox Marxism considered necessary for such a step, its insubstantial proletariat would require assistance from the peasantry (which could be mobilized by land reform) and from a highly organized and disciplined political party (the Bolsheviks) which would fight for its interests before it was even able to articulate them.

Lenin's view carried the day, despite political setbacks and opposition from many of his comrades, and the result was the Bolshevik takeover of 25 October (new style: 7 November) 1917. But seizing power, at a time of state breakdown and near-anarchy, was the easy bit: a much greater test would be holding on to it and making something of it.

By mid-1921, the Bolsheviks had defied the predictions of their opponents and managed to hang on through the Civil War. But that still left open the nature and the speed of the revolutionary transformation they were overseeing. Even the most utopian revolutionary could not deny that Russia was a long way off the proletarian republic that it was 'meant' to be. The communist ideal of a classless and conflict-free society lay a long way in the future. In the medium term – on this point Lenin and his comrades were unambiguous – the proletariat would exercise its dictatorship through the means of coercion it had inherited from the bourgeois state. The new regime made no apologies for discriminating against and persecuting the 'bourgeois' elements that were bound to remain hostile to the Soviet order. Nor did it leave any doubt that the proletariat would exercise its 'dictatorship' through a party whose leading members spent their formative years at a comfortable remove from the factory floor.

Nonetheless, this phase of proletarian dictatorship was far from being the end-point of history. Nikolai Bukharin and Evgeny Preobrazhensky's *ABC of Communism*, an extended gloss on the party programme of 1919 that was the most influential Bolshevik primer in the 1920s, looked forward to a time when the need for coercive measures would recede and the state would 'die out':

> There will be no need for special ministers of State, for police and prisons, for laws and decrees – nothing of the sort. Just as in an orchestra all the performers watch the conductor's baton and act accordingly, so here all will consult the statistical reports and will direct their work accordingly.

When exactly would all this happen? Here Bukharin and Preobrazhensky gestured towards the historical middle distance: 'Two or three generations of persons will have to grow up under the new conditions before the need will pass for laws and punishments and for the use of repressive measures by the workers' State. Not until then will all the vestiges of the capitalist past disappear.'

Bolshevik Marxism was a mixture of the scientific and the prophetic. On the one hand, it based its claims to legitimacy on purportedly rigorous and empirical study of economic and political trends. Lenin had earned his stripes in the Russian social-democratic movement in the 1890s through a close analysis of stratification and proto-capitalism among the Russian peasantry, and his later accounts of global imperialism also referred extensively to economic data. On the other hand, the Bolsheviks were making projections into the future that had little foundation in the present: how likely was it that the poor, hungry, ill-educated, fractious, and traumatized society that emerged from the Civil War would learn good habits and be able to dispense with the coercive functions of the state?

To take such predictions seriously, even as a dim and distant prospect, required a leap of faith and a concentrated effort of the collective imagination. Marxism-Leninism had to become not only the ideology of the ruling party but also the belief system of Soviet society; it had to become a political religion. Like proponents of other religions, the Bolsheviks made matters of belief inseparable from habits and behaviour. They tried to wrench Soviet people out of patterns of life and thought associated with the old regime. In early 1918, they hastened to implement a piece of legislation they had inherited from the Provisional Government: the Julian calendar of tsarist Russia was replaced by the Gregorian calendar, which meant a leap forward of 13 days. Measures were taken to whittle down the dozens of Orthodox holidays and to provide suitably revolutionary alternatives. The Bolshevik state quickly nationalized church land and removed the church's control over education, birth, and marriage.

If Soviet society retained some undesirable aspects (drunkenness, bribe-taking), these could be put down as 'remnants of the past' caused by the harshness and injustice of life before the Revolution. Opposition to the forward march of Soviet socialism was embodied by 'former people' such as those who had served as priests or policemen, or simply been 'bourgeois', before 1917. Manichean comparisons between 'then' and 'now' were a trusty rhetorical fallback of the regime in the 1920s and 1930s.

In a more proactive move, the Bolsheviks also strove to drive time forwards. In the mid-1920s, American efficiency and Taylorist management techniques were all the rage. In July 1923, a 'League of Time' was set up with the mission to reduce wasted time at the Soviet workplace. At one Moscow factory, activists reduced the time taken to hand out wages to workers from nearly 40 hours to just over one hour. Short-term goals alternated with longer-term visions of the future. Russian science fiction publications – many of them with an anti-capitalist dystopian edge – reached an unprecedented high of almost 50 in 1927 alone. Home-grown works were supplemented by around 200 translations of foreign works (especially Jules Verne and H. G. Wells).

Yet such futuristic visions were undermined by the fact that the Bolsheviks, according to their own terms, had taken a step back from historical progress. By making concessions to the peasantry in their 'New Economic Policy' of 1921, they had put the brakes on the proletarianization and economic development that were meant to be preconditions for Russia's leap to communism. Furious debates raged among the Bolsheviks about the desirability of this policy. What if it was just a backward step?

The debate was resolved in 1928, when the Soviet Union under Stalin set a course for breakneck industrialization. Before long the five-year plan was compressed into four years, and in February 1931 Stalin declared that it should be completed in three, in 'the basic and decisive branches of industry'. The ultimatum he delivered to his industrial managers could not have been more blunt. After centuries of taking 'continual beatings' from various foreigners – from the Mongols in the 13th century to the Japanese in the early 20th – Russia must now catch up or perish. As Stalin concluded: 'We are fifty or a hundred years behind the advanced countries. We must make good this distance in ten years. Either we do it, or we shall go under.'

This was an era when all the most promethean designs for accelerating history were given their head. The signature novel of the period, Valentin Kataev's *Time, Forward!* (1931–2), unfolded practically in real time as it plunged the reader into a single day in the life of a work team that is striving to break the record for mixing concrete in a single eight-hour shift. In the first scene, the main protagonist (the engineer who masterminds the record attempt) wakes ahead of his alarm clock – for he 'could not entrust to it so precious a thing as time' – and the pace is unrelenting for the following 300 pages.

The struggle with 'remnants of the past' reached a new level of intensity. A new law of April 1929 greatly reduced the scope for organized religion, and the Soviet authorities demanded the extraction of 25,000 tons of scrap metal from expropriated church bells in the nine months from October 1930. Around half of the churches active at the start of collectivization were closed.

Visions of the bright future began to take more vivid material form. The Soviet Union was proclaimed to be radically remaking its own environment. New cities sprang up, millions of people streamed into them, and the Soviet population was enjoined to look beyond the squalor and misery of early industrialization to catch glimpses of its own bright future of gleaming modernity. It was helped in this endeavour by the Soviet culture industry. The mass media were dedicated to producing visions of the true socialist society that lay just beyond the horizon of current social experience, or at least to draw people's attention to premonitions of socialism in the present. Literary luminaries and party ideology chiefs combined to formulate the new doctrine of Soviet culture, socialist realism, which required cultural producers to show life not as it was, but as it should be.

Writers and film-makers excelled themselves in carrying out this mission. They produced inspiring stories of criminals remade by collective labour, of workers vanquishing or converting weedy members of the 'bourgeoisie', and of explorers and aviators conquering the vast territory of the USSR. By the mid-1930s, the achievers of such exploits could also expect to be well rewarded for their efforts. But that was only a secondary consideration: as one slogan of the time had it, Soviet people were 'born to turn fairytale into reality'. The 'Soviet dream' was exemplified on screen by *The Radiant Path* (1940), whose heroine (played by Stalinist cinema's greatest star, Liubov Orlova) makes a dizzying ascent from maid to high-achieving weaver, and from there to engineer and deputy to the Supreme Soviet. Throughout the film, the distinction between reality and fantasy projection is hard to establish – and that is precisely the point.

It is wise to be sceptical as to how warmly the forward-looking ethos was welcomed among the population. Many people, as secret

1. The heroine of *The Radiant Path* receives congratulations after a feat of record-breaking productivity

police reports on chuntering in bread queues abundantly illustrate, would much rather have had more bread or lower prices than have added their spade of cement to the foundations of communism; as one punning quip would later put it, they felt themselves to be turning not fairytale (*skazka*) but Kafka into reality. But the primacy of the future was unquestioned in the culture of the time. All Soviet people were made aware of where they stood on the communist timeline that stretched from backwardness and benightedness to modernity and socialism. Peasant women from Central Asia were at one extreme, high-achieving young male workers at the other.

In 1936, the Stalinist regime served notice that the country had taken its first substantial step along the timeline. The new Soviet constitution of that year removed discriminatory measures against 'alien' elements such as priests and former 'bourgeois': now suffrage was to be universal and ballots were to be secret. The constitution also extended to the population as a whole an unprecedented set of social benefits: the rights to work, to education, to rest, to housing, to support in the case of sickness or old age. What all this implied was that the USSR was now a 'classless' society where the antagonism between former exploiters and exploited had been lifted. The phase of dictatorship had apparently come to an end, a development that was soon hailed by communist sympathizers in the West. The English socialist Sidney Webb chose a condescending metaphor that made few concessions to the Marxist-Leninist vernacular, but his meaning was clear: 'The child born in 1917 has come of age, and takes an adult place in the world. Development, far from having stopped, is still proceeding at a greater rate than before; but it is now the development of an adult, broadening into ever-wider circles and still rising towards its prime.'

The significance of the 1936 constitution does not lie in its truth-value. It stands in the same relationship to Soviet reality as *The Radiant Path*. Universal suffrage in a political system where there was only ever one candidate, and where that candidate's selection would be rigorously overseen by the party agencies, was a sham. Articles on the absence of discrimination, or the inviolability of the person, seem grotesque in the light of the mass terror campaign that was about to erupt. However, this was a political culture that obsessively monitored its own progress towards certain abstract and long-term goals and thus suggested they might eventually be reached. Soviet ideology did not allow leaders to go for too long without announcing the next epoch-making leap forward.

The death of Stalin in 1953 required an update on the Soviet Union's historical trajectory. Stalin was denounced by his successor, Nikita Khrushchev, in 1956, which meant that current leaders could not rely on the authority of their predecessor to indicate the direction of historical change. Instead, they drank once more from the wells of revolutionary utopianism, producing in 1961 a party programme – the first such document since 1919 – which declared that by 1980 'a communist society will in the main be built in the USSR'. The radiant future had by now become imminent. It was to be prefigured by remarkable Soviet achievements in the present. If in the early Soviet period space travel had been in the realm of science fiction, by the time of the revamped party programme it was a reality. Yuri Gagarin's flight of 12 April 1961 turned him into the greatest Soviet icon of the post-Stalin era.

Moscow Does Not Believe in Tears

Directed by Vladimir Menshov in 1979, *Moscow Does Not Believe in Tears* won the Academy Award for Best Foreign Language Film in 1980. It tells the story of three girls who arrive in Moscow from the provinces in the late 1950s. One of them is a trouser-chaser determined to gain admission to the smart set and find herself a suitably glamorous and affluent man. Another is honest and stolid and quickly settles down with a husband of like temperament and values. The third – the heroine Katya – has the misfortune to be made pregnant by a spoiled scion of the Moscow elite. The first half of the film ends with her a distraught single mother. The second half zips forward 20 years: Katya is now a self-possessed factory director with a modern flat of her own and a well-adjusted grown-up daughter. All she lacks is the right man, and naturally she finds him. The film's international success is best explained by its instantly recognizable formula: a modern-day fairytale where rags become riches and adversity gives way to triumph (even if more emphasis is placed on the heroine's career success than would ever be the case in a Hollywood romance). But this fairytale is far more historically saturated than its Western counterparts: it presents a story of postwar progress, inviting Soviet viewers to reflect on the distance their country has travelled from the dormitory inhabited by the girls in the 1950s to the separate apartment Katya enjoys as a mature adult.

On closer inspection, however, the 1961 programme represented rather more than a technologically updated version of its 1919 predecessor. One meaningful difference was that Soviet leaders were much less nebulous in their prediction of what the future communist society might entail, and less vague about when it might be achieved. Some utopian rhetoric remained, but the essence of the socialist state was a modern welfare state along with increased material prosperity. Axioms of Soviet Marxism in its 1919 variant – the need to do away with price, credit, wage inequality, and specialization of labour – could now be downplayed or jettisoned in the interests of rapid economic growth. Yet at the same time the authors of the new programme could not resist ultra-ambitious projections: agricultural output would increase by a factor of 3.5, they said, though previous experience suggested this was a pipe-dream.

Another distinction lay in the frame of reference applied to Soviet achievements. Now the primary justification of the Soviet regime was not where it was going but how far it had come: life might be less fine than in America, but it still represented a large, even astounding, improvement on the situation in 1921 or 1945. This was a low-key message for a messianic Marxist regime, and one that could not be expected to resonate well with those citizens (well over a third of the population) too young to remember World War II, let alone the Civil War.

While the future had briefly seemed close at hand in a phase of technological utopianism in the early 1960s, it then slipped away again into the hazy middle distance. The sense of time as dynamic onward motion had almost totally dissipated by the 1970s. This was evident on an everyday level. Time was more open-ended for Soviet people, largely because it did not correlate to money as neatly as it did in the West. A two-day weekend was finally introduced in the Soviet Union in the late 1960s, which meant that people's lives were governed to an even greater extent by the patterns of family life and informal socializing. More relaxed work discipline made time theft at work a fact of Soviet life to an extent that pre-war Bolsheviks would have abhorred. As the Moscow correspondent of *The Times* commented of the late Brezhnev period: 'Life in the Soviet Union is so slow-moving, so settled in its pattern and framework that it would take a political earthquake to make even a slight jolt in the habits and thinking of Russians.' This once revolutionary society had by all appearances become stuck in its ways.

Looking back

But the main challenge to the forward-looking Soviet mentality came not from the present but from the past. Although the Soviet regime claimed legitimacy from the future to which it strove, it was no different from any other political order in that it also needed to present a credible account of its origins. The Bolsheviks set to work on this task immediately after coming precariously to power in 1917. The first anniversary of the October Revolution in 1918 was an elaborate affair, and it was preceded by celebrations to mark the

1905 Revolution (22 January), the Fall of the Autocracy (12 March), and the Paris Commune (18 March). In April 1918, the Bolshevik government ordered the replacement of tsarist monuments (except those classified as national treasures) with revolutionary equivalents. In 1920, on the third anniversary, the Bolsheviks staged a re-enactment of the storming of the Winter Palace. The spectacle had 8,000 participants (far in excess of the numbers actually involved in the events of 25–26 October 1917) and an audience of 100,000 (about a quarter of the city's population). It was a theatrical triumph, compressing the action into an hour and a half and using searchlights to direct the audience's attention. Here was a Russian Bastille: a symbolic centre for the revolution, a place that was at once real and mythical.

The creation of this revolutionary iconography was far from an automatic process. For one thing, the Bolshevik re-staging of the storming of the Winter Palace bore little relation to the event as it actually occurred. An even greater problem was that, although the Bolsheviks might claim to have seized power in Petrograd on the night of 7 November 1917, their consolidation of power in the rump Russian empire had depended on a great deal of uneasy collaboration with other socialist groups – and, as these other socialists would assert as loudly as the Bolsheviks permitted them, on the usurpation of the broader revolutionary socialist cause. What took place during the 1920s was a rapid 'Bolshevizing' of revolutionary memory. Committees were set up around the country to gather material for an authoritative 'History of the Party'; leading questions and editorial amendments ensured that local variations and ideological heresies would be written out of the story. In order to provide themselves with a suitable lineage, the Bolsheviks went back further in time – to the 1905 Revolution, to the worker circles of the 1890s, and to the entire 'revolutionary movement' of the last third of the 19th century. All these historical phenomena were now seen to have their teleological culmination in October 1917.

The celebrations of the tenth anniversary of the Revolution in 1927 confirmed the new orthodoxy.

In the 1930s, the Soviet Union became even more historically minded, and it increasingly favoured a kind of history that would

ОКТЯБРЬ

2. Scene from Eisenstein's *October*: Lenin (played by Vasilii Nikandrov) delivers a fiery speech on his arrival at the Finland Station in April 1917

have alienated Marx, Engels, and even Lenin. Accounts that presented history as the interplay of impersonal economic forces fell into disrepute. What took over was the kind of 'Great Men' approach which – stripped of some perfunctory references to 'feudal absolutism' and the like – would not have been out of place in a Victorian classroom. As Stalin put it at the end of 1931, 'Marxism has never denied the role of heroes'.

Far from coincidentally, this was also the time when the Soviet Union was developing a Russian-dominated state-centred patriotism to replace the Marxist internationalism that had earlier been its watchword. Great men and battles stirred the blood in a way that base and superstructure clearly did not. By now Peter the Great could be enlisted as a worthy precursor of the Bolsheviks for his commitment to expanding and bolstering the state. The most eloquent pre-revolutionary recruit to the Soviet cause was Ivan the Terrible. From about 1937 onwards, the notorious cruelty of this 16th-century ruler was downplayed in favour of his achievements in gathering together various principalities in a strong Muscovite state. Sergei Eisenstein was one of several major cultural figures to be set the task of rehabilitating Ivan. Early in 1941, the famous director received straight from the Kremlin a commission for a film on this subject; he worked on the project through wartime evacuation in Kazakhstan. Part One of the film (completed 1944) won a Stalin Prize, but Part Two (1946) received a severe reprimand and was shelved. Stalin took the director to task for having depicted the tsar as a vacillating 'Hamlet' rather than a resolute state-builder, and his army was shown as no better than the 'Klu Klux Klan'. Eisenstein's travails revealed all the difficulties of reappropriating the pre-revolutionary past.

Another reason for the mobilization of such patriotic myths was that the Soviet Union felt itself well in advance of 1941 to be on a war footing. When the German invasion took place, the search for comforting historical parallels became all the more urgent. Almost immediately, the conflict was christened the 'Great Patriotic War'.

3. Scene from *Ivan the Terrible*: Ivan surveys his people marching to beg him to restore order in Muscovy

Soviet culture became overtly backward-looking in its search for moral succour at a time of emergency. Comparisons with the first Patriotic War – the campaign against Napoleon in 1812–14 – were a staple of war journalism. The struggle with Nazi Germany was also widely referred to as a 'holy war', and this was not just a turn of phrase. The regime put a stop to anti-religious propaganda and permitted a few churches to reopen; in September 1943, moreover, Stalin received church leaders in the Kremlin and agreed to the convocation of a church council to elect a patriarch.

After the defeat of Nazi Germany, the war entered the realm of patriotic memory. Soviet society had another heroic point of reference – one that rivalled and perhaps even supplanted the Revolution itself. The war had the advantage of being more inclusive and less divisive than the formative years of the Soviet Union. At the time of the October Revolution, the Bolshevik Party had only 350,000 members; many of these were dead by 1945. The Red Army in May 1945 numbered well over 11 million men, from an elastic age range of 18 to 55. Although ethnic groups that had suffered deportation or forced incorporation into the USSR had every reason to opt out of the patriotic Soviet account of World War II, many people found it accommodated them. Veterans as a group received few favours from the Soviet state in the first decade

4. Newlyweds lay a wreath at the Tomb of the Unknown Soldier at the Kremlin wall, Moscow, 9 May 1974

after the war, but the suffering and sacrifices of the 'war generation' started to become a more public matter in the late 1950s, while the Brezhnev period saw a full-blown cult of the Great Patriotic War. Victory Day was re-established as a public holiday in 1965, thousands of war memorials went up, and material benefits and decorations were lavished on veterans.

The Great Patriotic War delivered a great boost to the historical legitimacy of the Soviet order, but for a heavily ideological regime obsessed with matters of doctrine, this was not enough. Nikita Khrushchev's decision to expose Stalin's crimes against his own party in a 'secret speech' to the 20th Party Congress in 1956 brought a renewed crisis of historical memory. How was the Soviet Union to redefine its historical myths, given that so many of them had grown alongside the cult of the deceased dictator?

The solution, as ever, was to return to Lenin: to assert that the leader of the Revolution represented an unblemished Bolshevik ethos that was subsequently distorted by the 'cult of personality' under Stalin. But in fact the first and most enduring cult of personality had been that of Lenin. From 1918 onwards, adulation of the Bolshevik leader had become *de rigueur*, and by the time of his final incapacitation in 1923 'Leninism' was synonymous with the party line at any given moment. To the distaste of some old Bolsheviks, Lenin's death was the cue for a cult with numerous material trappings: monuments, artefacts (from teacups to cigarette boxes), and in due course the dead leader's body. The extraordinary notion that Lenin should be permanently exhibited in a communist shrine soon took hold, and the famous mausoleum on Red Square went up in 1930.

Yet, although the 50th anniversary of the Revolution (1967) and the 100th of Lenin's birth (1970) were celebrated with much pomp, the later Soviet period saw the revival of memory of a less explicitly revolutionary nature. One point was that the Great Patriotic War established itself even more firmly as the most meaningful historical marker for the Soviet population. Another was that the regime of Leonid Brezhnev (General Secretary 1964–82) took several steps back from Nikita Khrushchev's de-Stalinization. Criticism of Stalin could now be interpreted as an unhealthy fixation on moral questions at the expense of national and state considerations. While Soviet people knew quite well about Stalin's terror, they could also be encouraged to think of the dictator as a leader who used (often rightly) cruel means to defend the interests of the Soviet state and to build a just society. In time-honoured fashion, 'excesses' could be put down to the ways in which his comrades misled him or distorted his instructions.

In addition, the Soviet Union, like any reasonably mature industrial society, was seeking the firm ground of tradition. Soviet people attached more importance to their own life cycle than to the historical future of the Soviet Union, and the government was willing to recognize this. The first 'Wedding Palace' opened for business in 1959 in Leningrad, and by 1972 the Soviet Union had 600 such institutions. For the educated urban population it became fashionable to acquire antique furniture and to trawl the provinces in search of the 'heritage' of villages, churches, and elderly peasants. A new literary movement named 'village prose' provided, at its best, moving and poetic depictions of a rural world that the Soviet Union had come close to destroying. Some public figures even got away with subjecting the Revolution to creeping reinterpretation as a national tragedy rather than an unqualified triumph – though they were more inclined to blame Jews and foreigners for its excesses than the Bolshevik Party.

By the 1970s, it was hard to escape the feeling that this revolutionary regime had become conservative and backward-looking. This was evident at the summit of the party-state hierarchy, which was showing all the signs of gerontocracy: the 'Brezhnev generation', born in the first decade of the 20th century, which had got its first big break at the time of the Great Terror in the 1930s, was clinging on to the top political jobs in its dotage.

The idea of youth as the vanguard of social transformation, which had always been heavily promoted by the Soviet regime, was no longer so plausible. The great expansion of the Communist Youth League (Komsomol) – to 40 million young people by the mid-1980s – was bought at the expense of its ideological fervour.

The past unravels: the Gorbachev era

The next bold initiative in Soviet history – Mikhail Gorbachev's perestroika, or 'restructuring' – was designed to counteract the impression that the Soviet Union was running out of steam. This reform programme was supposed to revitalize the Soviet Union and give it a fresh push along the road to a bright future. Some of its goals were modest: to do battle with perennial Soviet problems such as alcoholism and slack work discipline. Others, however, sounded more ambitious: Gorbachev spoke of instilling 'new thinking' and unleashing the 'human factor'.

The social and political implications of these woolly notions were unclear, probably even to Gorbachev himself. In the event, the Soviet population could not be roused to another big collective effort. The state no longer had effective means of coercion at its disposal. Society did not respond to the initiatives as it was supposed to. Even youth, supposedly the vanguard of social and political change, let Gorbachev down: the Komsomol of the late 1980s was a breeding ground for entrepreneurs, not for true believers. And the political changes that Gorbachev found himself instigating – partially contested elections in 1989 – were such as to undermine the sacred political value of the Soviet Union: the monopoly on power of the party-state.

Instead of pointing the way to a radiant Soviet future, perestroika led to an accelerated reckoning with the past. It had started on the familiar ideological territory of 'Leninism'. In 1987, the 70th anniversary of the Revolution was celebrated as if early Bolshevism contained an uncorrupted core of socialism that the Soviet Union, whatever its tragedies and crises, had carried through to the late 20th century. Over the next four years, however, the historical revelations escalated as Soviet society took up the discussion that had been terminated a few years after Khrushchev's de-Stalinizing speech of 1956. Soviet people learned that Stalin's crimes had been not only against party members but against all manner of other people as well. His regime had directly caused the mass starvation of the peasantry in the early 1930s. It had been responsible for the killing of more than 20,000 Polish POWs in 1940, a crime that the Soviets had always publicly blamed on the Germans but finally admitted to 50 years after the event. With the publication in 1990 of the secret protocols to the Molotov–Ribbentrop Pact of 1939, Stalin was revealed to have been in cahoots with Hitler on the very eve of the Great Patriotic War. Worse still for the Soviet system, in 1989–90 Russian historians began to take aim at the hitherto untouchable subjects: Marxism, Leninism, and the Revolution itself.

The revelations were also literary. Previously unmentionable names were restored to the Soviet reading public in a great rush. In 1990, for example, Soviet people could be seen devouring Nabokov's *Lolita*, Solzhenitsyn's *Gulag Archipelago*, and Orwell's *Nineteen Eighty-Four*: three contrasting works of literature that were somehow made equivalent by their status as banned in the Soviet period. In the Soviet Union between 1987 and 1991, history (whether political, social, or cultural) became a mass political issue in a way that it has probably never been at any other time and in any other place. The implications for even a relatively liberal Soviet leadership were troubling: how could Gorbachev cling to the idea of a legitimate Soviet order when historical sources were showing that the regime had been murderous from the very beginning?

The avalanche of historical revelations, along with the turbulence of the Soviet collapse, called into question the Soviet model of time as linear progress along a historical timeline. By 1991, other spatial metaphors for Russian history seemed more convincing: a full circle from one despotism to another, or from one revolution to another; an endless cycle of reform and reaction; a meandering into obsolescence; or simply a dead-end.

Almost 20 years on from the collapse of the Soviet Union, most Russians would say that these assessments are unduly dismissive of the Soviet experience. It is true that the October Revolution is by now close to an irrelevance. When Russians look to an historical event in the Soviet period to stir their blood, they think above all of the Great Patriotic War. When people of a certain age are asked when life was best for them in the Soviet period, they mostly mention the Brezhnev period of stable prices and modest but respectable living standards (the hardships and aggravations of Soviet life in the 1970s have largely faded from the memory).

Such assessments draw our attention to a central irony of the uniquely forward-looking Soviet civilization. The USSR was brought into being by a group of revolutionaries who constantly professed communism as their ultimate goal. This fundamental orientation towards the future never disappeared, though it often went out of focus. At the same time, however, the Soviet Union was gaining more and more of a past: its own history, its own traditions, generations of people who had been socialized as 'Soviet'. The need to point simultaneously forwards to a radiant future and backwards to a heroic past led to ideological contortions: how, after all, was a society obliged to pay obeisance to 1917 to keep in step with the rapid changes of the 20th century? Eventually, in the Soviet Union as in other societies, most people found their most useful point of reference not in prospective Marxist stages of development but in the near past of living memory and recent experience and the distant past of stories of common origins. In present-day Russia, for better or worse, the Soviet Union has found its niche in just such a story.

Chapter 2
Coercion and participation

Political violence has always been recognized as crucial to the functioning of the Soviet state, especially in the first few decades of its existence. 'Ordinary' Soviet people have traditionally been seen as its helpless victims. Yet this notion overlooks another notable aspect of the Soviet system: the fact that it demanded – and received – an unprecedented level of participation from its citizens. Soviet people cast votes, read newspapers, served in the army and the KGB, took part in meetings, and denounced each other. How sustainable, in this light, is the distinction between a small group of party-state predators and an oppressed 'society'? Were the individual and 'the regime' always at loggerheads, or might they work in tandem?

The evolution of Soviet terror

The idea of using extreme violence to achieve objectives was never alien to the Bolsheviks. In the late summer of 1918, following a failed uprising by the rival Socialist Revolutionaries and an unsuccessful attempt to assassinate Lenin, they unleashed a campaign of 'Red Terror'. Opponents were rounded up; tens of thousands were summarily executed, and tens of thousands more interned in the first Soviet concentration camps. The families of deserters were taken hostage. Even the groups who were meant to be the beneficiaries of revolution were beaten down if they stepped out of line. In early 1921, an uprising by the sailors of Kronstadt, just across the water from the citadel of Bolshevik power, was put down within a couple of weeks at a cost of thousands of casualties.

In the Bolsheviks' defence it might be said that civil wars are always savage and that their opponents were just as ready to kill to defend their cause. But there are a number of reasons to treat the Bolshevik case as something qualitatively different. One is their apparatus of violence: a mere six weeks after their seizure of power they set up an Extraordinary Commission for Combating Counter-Revolution and Sabotage (Cheka), which acquired judicial and executive functions early in 1918. As its name suggests, this institution was first viewed as a temporary expedient, but it proved far too useful to be dispensed with. In 1922, it was incorporated into the Ministry of Internal Affairs (NKVD), and its successor organizations would bear various names (including, from 1954, 'Committee for State Security', or KGB). But the underlying principle – that socialist 'democracy' needed constant support from instruments of coercion accountable to no one but the top leadership – never changed.

The Bolsheviks were unapologetic, even proud, to be waging a campaign of 'terror'. For them, this word had an admirable revolutionary pedigree; in any case, their self-image insisted that to turn away from violence was to display woeful lack of political resolve. No less revealing is the fact that, from the very beginning of their terror campaign, they were ready to identify people as hostile not for what they had done but for who they were. If people were 'bourgeois', they were *ipso facto* 'enemies' and worse. The Bolshevik elite had no compunction in demanding 'merciless mass terror' against groups deemed to be counter-revolutionary, and in specifying exactly how the policy was to be carried out. The language and the mindset of the subsequent terror campaigns were already in place. State-orchestrated violence would remain a central feature of Soviet life for the next 30 years.

The Soviet regime can thus be seen to have waged war on its own people for several decades. The atmosphere of combat was heightened by the acute social upheaval of forced collectivization and industrialization, and by the fact that society was in any case on a permanent war footing due to fears of capitalist encirclement and aggression. In the first half of the 1940s, the Soviet Union was at war with a real external enemy, and after a brief enemyless interlude in 1945–6, the lines of a new, 'cold', war were drawn.

In one sense, however, all subsequent instances of state-sponsored violence differed from their Civil War precursors: they were not identified by the Soviet regime itself as 'terror' (though this term was readily applied by the victims and by commentators outside the USSR). This change in usage reflected in part the sense that a supposedly proletarian state, once it had secured power, should not be terrorizing its population, but also the fact that the targets of violence had changed character. From the late 1920s onwards, 'enemies' were located within, not outside, Soviet society. Most of the violence on Soviet soil was perpetrated not by conflicting sides that constituted separate armies and political organizations but by the subjects of a one-party state. The Bolsheviks operated an extreme variant of 'us and them' ideology; for those excluded from the Soviet community, the consequences could be terrifying. But the criteria for social exclusion and physical elimination were often opaque. Unlike Nazi Germany, where racial considerations were always paramount, it was often hard to say who 'we' were and who 'they' might be.

Even if we limit ourselves to the infamous political violence of 1937–8, it can be seen that there was not one Terror but multiple terrors. Early accounts of these events tended to concentrate on their most visible victims: the leading Bolsheviks, Stalin's former comrades, who were convicted in major show trials between 1936 and 1938, and the relatively few people, mostly members of the intelligentsia, who left memoirs of their terrible experiences. While the Terror always had an arbitrary quality, it is clear enough what characteristics placed such people at risk: foreign travel or acquaintance with foreigners, previous brushes with 'Trotskyism' or other ideological deviations, or the patronage of those exposed as 'enemies of the people'. More recent, archivally based studies have broadened the social portrait of the Terror, drawing attention to the fact that the violence of 1937–8 came as the culmination of an extended period of disorder following collectivization. Stalin's war on the peasantry had brought a surge in robbery, hooliganism, black market activity, and vagrancy. Some dekulakized peasants had taken up arms: in 1933, 35 armed bandit gangs were reported to be at large in the Urals region. Military units and special political police forces struggled to contain the unrest. Mass arrests in rural areas tailed off after 1933, but the centre of police activity shifted to the city, where millions of desperate and hungry peasants had fled. In 1935, police operations in the Russian republic alone brought the arrest of 266,000 people identified as 'socially dangerous elements'. When violence escalated in 1937 and 1938, old categories of public enemy – 'kulaks', 'recidivists', 'marginals' – could be revisited. Following the Politburo's introduction of arrest and execution quotas in August 1937, branches of the NKVD had every incentive to go looking for 'anti-Soviet elements' in all the usual places. The introduction of internal passports in 1932 had created ideal conditions for their operation: now the documents could reveal in an instant whether an arrestee was 'socially harmful' and subject to expulsion.

But that still leaves the question of why it happened. How could a society have succumbed to this madness? How could it have ended up seeing enemies everywhere?

Stalin was probably the only person to understand the full scale of what was happening, and he was certainly the only person who could have brought it to an end. His responsibility for raising the tempo of terror – notably through the infamous order no. 00447 of August 1937 that imposed arrest quotas – is absolutely clear.

But even Stalin was sending out signals rather than directing every stage of the terror process; and even he seems to have been surprised (though not displeased) by the scale and intensity of the violence.

A structural answer to the question of the origins of the Terror would draw attention to the workings of the Soviet state. The USSR had a formidable institutional apparatus of violence, which its leaders were not slow to use. They subscribed to a purportedly scientific theory of the management of society according to which rogue elements needed to be isolated and transformed – or, if not transformed, then eliminated. Not only were state agencies primed to arrest and imprison refractory citizens, there was also an impressive 'shadow' bureaucracy whose role was to supervise the regular state agencies and to sniff out malfeasance and political unreliability. In addition to the political police and the procuracy, there was (until 1934) a 'Worker-Peasant Inspectorate'. These various organizations fought among themselves for resources and legitimacy, hurling back and forth accusations that would provide much fuel for the conflagration of terror in the late 1930s.

Another point is that there were plenty of problems in 1930s Russia, and plenty of reasons to look for scapegoats. Hastily installed machinery broke down. Tools were sub-standard and in short supply. Fires, explosions, and workplace accidents took place with suspicious frequency. Workers remained poorly housed and underfed, and a poor harvest in 1936 placed further strain on the provisioning system. Overwrought industrial managers desperately struck deals with each other to guarantee an adequate supply of scarce resources. Some of the methods they employed to fulfil their plans shaded into out-and-out corruption.

But, to explain adequately the explosion of violence in the Soviet 1930s, we need to probe more deeply the political culture of Bolshevism. The military ethos of the Civil War period lived on in the Bolshevik elite of the 1930s. This was truly a party that felt itself

5. Poster 'Long Live the NKVD', 1939. Political violence is here depicted in terms reminiscent of a folk tale: as a struggle between righteous valour and bestial evil

to be at war – effectively against its own society, though it did not put it that way. The mindset was expressed early in 1933 by Nikolai Bukharin, a particularly valuable witness as he is sometimes considered to be the civilized face of Bolshevism and was to fall victim to the last of the major show trials of the 1930s: 'we must march onward, shoulder to shoulder, in battle formation, sweeping aside all vacillations with the utmost Bolshevik ruthlessness, hacking off all factions, which can only serve to reflect vacillations within the country'.

This gory metaphor is, however, somewhat misleading: the party was expecting not to engage in open combat with a declared enemy but to smoke out fifth columnists. In its origins it was a conspiratorial organization, and in its development as a ruling regime it had institutionalized suspicion of its own members and of society at large. Party members were periodically called on to account for themselves before 'purge commissions'. Those outside the party would find their commitment to the cause interrogated in other ways – if they were unlucky, in the cells of the NKVD. It was as if all members of Soviet society were guilty until proved innocent – and innocence could not be proved once and for all, but had continually to be demonstrated anew through deeds rather than words. The imperative of self-justification (and often self-reinvention) was all the more acute because most Soviet people had a past that was in some way vulnerable: in the 1930s, the existence of a 'kulak' or 'bourgeois' relative was quite enough to sabotage the life chances of even an exemplary Soviet citizen.

Interwar Bolshevism was therefore unlike other authoritarian political systems where the population could at least sit tight and do nothing to draw attention to itself. The categories of victim in the USSR were so arbitrary and so variable that keeping one's head down was no guarantee of safety. To have been present when an anti-Soviet joke was told – without rebuking the joker or reporting the incident – could be enough to condemn a person to the Gulag or worse. And, even when an 'enemy' had been identified and locked away, the rationale for incarceration was not simply to punish but to extend to prisoners the opportunity to redeem themselves through slave labour on construction projects or in sub-Arctic mines. For inmates of the Gulag, this distinction was perhaps of little interest, but it marks out most Soviet repression from most Nazi terror, whose aim was to destroy racially defined enemies (in the process extracting economic value from them).

The soviets and popular mobilization

The Stalinist political system was designed to mobilize the population, to keep it in a perpetual state of readiness for whatever superhuman challenges history might put in its way. Soviet people were expected to be active participants, not slaves. The ethos of grass-roots participation was present even in the title of the country: the 'soviets' were popularly elected councils that had first formed during the revolution of 1905. After the February Revolution of 1917, they again sprang up in all manner of environments: factories, army units, villages. The larger soviets in the major cities (especially Petrograd) quickly became powerful, if unruly, institutions. They stood in a tense and uncertain relationship to the 'Provisional Government' that was filled mainly with pre-revolutionary parliamentarians. By the summer of 1917, the slogan of 'soviet power' – based on the notion that popularly elected soviets should take over government – was gaining force. The problem, however, was that the soviets did not represent a coherent or structured set of political interests: they accommodated several socialist parties and factions, as well as plenty of people who followed no party line.

In September 1917, the Bolsheviks gained control of the powerful Petrograd soviet, and used this power base in the capital to take over government by force. As soviets turned into institutions of revolutionary government, their working practices became altogether less democratic than the revolutionary ideal of a popular assembly. Even before the Bolshevik takeover, the working life of the soviets was hived off into committees, sub-committees, and smoke-filled rooms. After October, the soviets were soon overshadowed by other institutions: above all, the Bolshevik Party, which during the Civil War period assumed a close supervisory role.

The reality of Bolshevik takeover of purportedly democratic institutions was all too clear. But the notion of popular participation remained important to the self-understanding of the USSR. The 1936 constitution proclaimed the democratic nature of the Soviet state: suffrage was now universal (where there had previously been class restrictions), and voting took place by secret ballot (where it had often previously been conducted by show of hands at meetings). The publication of the constitution and the staging of elections to the Supreme Soviet the following year were accompanied by an 18-month frenzy of publicity. Although each ballot had only one candidate, local officials tried their utmost to get people out to vote, and election statistics proclaimed a turnout of 98.61%.

6. Revolution Day, Moscow, 7 November 1978. A key ritual of popular participation

The legitimacy of Soviet rule depended on constant manifestations of popular enthusiasm. Rituals of involvement included not only voting, but also parades, meetings, and even carnivals. Nor was participation to become merely a matter of routine. The authorities were constantly mobilizing people for new feats of endurance and dedication. By engaging in 'socialist competition', citizens could demonstrate their devotion to the cause and their sterling qualities. The 'campaign' was close to the standard mode of operation for Soviet people from the late 1920s to World War II and beyond.

To dismiss these forms of mass mobilization as mere coercion is to obscure one important point. In the interwar the Soviet Union (and not only there), democracy never purported to be liberal; it was quite compatible with dictatorship. To a Soviet ear, democracy in a Western understanding connoted social injustice, division, and the rule of special interests. In the Soviet Union, by contrast, *demokratiya* both acted out the laws of history and represented the concerted and organized expression of the popular will. The interests of the 'toiling masses' were not watered down by 'bourgeois' parliamentary institutions but rather acted out by the Bolshevik state. The start of the Great Terror and the election campaign of 1937 together reinforced the notion, crucial to the legitimacy of the Soviet order, that extreme violence could be 'popular' (meaning 'of the people').

There is also hard evidence that repression could be 'popular' in the more common sense of the word. In 1928, when a group of engineers and technical specialists in the Donbass region of the Ukraine faced the death penalty in the first terror-style show trial, many Moscow workers thought the punishment too lenient (53 defendants, only 5 executions). Part of the momentum of the 1930s terror campaign was built by setting disgruntled workers against scapegoated industrial managers. More generally, Soviet violence in the 1930s depended on a huge amount of popular participation in the form of denunciation. To be a secret police informant was practically obligatory in certain lines of work – the upper echelons of the Church hierarchy, for example. But, in Soviet culture, denunciation could be presented more positively as whistle-blowing. In a speech of May 1928, Stalin stated that, if a worker had a complaint to make against a manager, it should be made even if it was only 5 or 10% true. Pavlik Morozov, a peasant boy from the Urals who was murdered in 1932, supposedly because he had denounced his own father as a kulak, became for a while a model for Soviet children.

The Polish historian Jan T. Gross has given perhaps the most powerful account of how the Soviet regime might set one group of people against another. In his study of the Soviet occupation of eastern Poland between 1939 and 1941, Gross shows how the majority Ukrainian population were effectively given a free hand in expressing their resentment at the minority (but, on the whole, wealthier) Polish population. In the early days of the occupation, the Red Army actively incited violence against the 'bloodsucking' Polish landowners. Thereafter, local vigilantes were able to get themselves appointed as the militia; arbitrary violence and formal authority worked in partnership. Contrary to many conventional notions of the totalitarian state as striving for omniscience and control, this was a society without firm rules where everyone had the right of appeal to higher authority to gain advantage over their neighbours. The problem, however, was that everyone was vulnerable to similar appeals being made against them. What took place, in Gross's words, was 'the induced self-destruction of a community'. We are left with a disturbing picture of a totalitarian regime not as an all-seeing executioner but as a slovenly and inhumane prison guard who leaves the inmates to fight a Hobbesian war of all against all, knowing that he can intervene with decisive effect in any particular conflict.

The case of occupied Poland was an extreme example. In the Soviet Union proper, it was more conceivable that participation might express true conviction rather than ethnic animosity or material envy. Soviet diaries that have come to light since the fall of communism have proved that in the 1930s there were Soviet people – primarily young, urban, and male – who strove to bring their thoughts and actions into line with Bolshevik ideals. The zeal of some of these enthusiasts was conditioned by a sense of their own inadequacy or vulnerability: perhaps they had a kulak father or a factory-owning grandfather. Many others had every incentive to support a regime that offered them education, excitement, and decent career prospects; the 1930s cohort often achieved rapid promotion over the bodies of the victims of the Terror.

Most Soviet people in the 1930s were, however, too busy to write diaries or too prudent to leave them to posterity. What can we know about their attitudes? Were they collaborating, wholeheartedly participating, dissenting, resisting? One of the many drawbacks of a violent dictatorship is that it has few ways of gauging popular opinion. Among the few sources are secret police reports on the popular mood, which reveal a good deal of everyday dissatisfaction. The great majority of Soviet people experienced hard times in the 1930s even if they did not suffer arrest or exile. There was plenty of

Letter from mother to son, July 1941

My dear son Lyonya! I am addressing you and all your comrades in the tank crews. Smash the bloodthirsty enemy like a dog, show him no mercy. My dear son, your father was a partisan. During the civil war his enemies exacted bestial punishment on him. They wounded him 21 times and gouged his eyes out. Hundreds of fighters died with him.

When your father was buried, I vowed that his son would avenge the blood of his father. Now the hour of retribution has come. I am proud that I have raised a son who's a fighter. Son, make sure you smash the fascist scum, smash him mercilessly!

This letter is preserved in the archive of Leningrad Radio. During the war, Soviet people were invited to send in letters to and from loved ones so that these could be read out on air. Tens of thousands of listeners responded, and the rubric 'Letters to and from the Front' became a fixture in wartime programming. The letters vary in tone and preoccupations, but they all show ordinary Soviet people adding their own emotional resonance to the patriotic cause. This letter reminds us that wartime patriotism was not only a matter of heroic self-defence and self-sacrifice but also an outlet for the rage, frustration, and violence endemic in Soviet society.

discontent for police informants to report back from bread queues. But the evidence suggests that, by the 1930s, few urban people were inclined to question the basic legitimacy of the Soviet regime (the collectivized village, where millions had died and many more were displaced and impoverished, was a very different matter).

State and society, 1941–64

The Great Patriotic War temporarily simplified the relationship between coercion and participation. The terror came primarily from an external enemy, while participation could be judged more unambiguously in terms of contribution to the war effort. That still left millions of people unfairly stigmatized: those who had had the misfortune to live in German-occupied territory and had failed to join the armed resistance, those who had fallen into captivity, and those who were deemed to belong to 'traitor peoples' such as the Chechens or the Volga Germans (the descendants of 18th-century German migrants to central Russia). But tens of millions more fought the war and assessed the cause on terms that differed relatively little from those employed by the regime.

The period 1945 to 1953 is often considered to be the most dismal phase of Stalinist dictatorship, but in one respect it was milder than the 1930s: there was no repeat of the bacchanalia of terror in 1937–8. The political police became a more cold-blooded and pragmatic organization, making greater use of professional agents at the expense of 'spontaneous' denunciations. With the exception of purges of the Leningrad party and state planning organizations in 1949, there was no bloodletting in the upper political elite. The signs were that the Soviet system was becoming stable and hierarchical in a way that it had not been before the war. The historian Cynthia Hooper has drawn from this a provocative conclusion: 'the Soviet state that emerged from the Second World War resembled that of its fascist enemy far more than it ever had in the 1930s'.

Soviet power still had plenty of targets and victims, but they were now defined less ambiguously. After a mass amnesty in 1945, the Gulag population was replenished by inmates arrested on criminal charges, many of them under draconian 1947 legislation on 'theft of socialist property', an offence that carried a minimum sentence of 7 years and a maximum of 25. From 1946 to 1952, just under half a million people were convicted of political crimes, the vast majority of them ending up in a labour camp. But around 10 times that number were put in prison or camps for 'ordinary' criminal convictions. If we add in other categories of victim (young people conscripted into labour battalions, POWs instantly rearrested on their return to the Soviet Union, exiled or imprisoned national groups), it becomes clear that there was no lessening of repression in postwar Russia – just that repression was more securely harnessed by party-state agencies.

In due course, however, the regime faced a major threat to the stability of this postwar arrangement. Within weeks of Stalin's death, his successors began to release prisoners from the camps. The first wave of amnesties set free well over a million people, or almost 50% of the Gulag population. If in the 1930s social turbulence had been caused by denunciations and arrests, in the mid-1950s the destabilizing factor was release and 'rehabilitation'. Then, in 1956, Khrushchev publicly denounced the terror that had occurred in the Stalin era. As previously, the regime sought to mobilize the Soviet population for the cause of building socialism, but it now had to do so without the draconian measures of the 1930s. Could mass participation in the Soviet enterprise be induced without terror?

One time-honoured Soviet method of eliciting participation was to announce a flagship project. In the Khrushchev era this was the Virgin Lands campaign, a programme to boost Soviet agricultural production by exploiting vast areas of steppe in Kazakhstan and Western Siberia for grain cultivation. By mid-March 1954, within

7. **Space pilot Yuri Gagarin and his wife cast their votes in the election to the USSR Supreme Soviet, 1962**

10 days of the party plenum that had announced the initiative, almost 25,000 volunteers had been despatched. The total Komsomol recruitment over the period 1954–60 was more than 360,000. Between 1954 and 1958, the Virgin Landers took over 40 million hectares of uncultivated land and raised grain production in the USSR by more than one-third.

Another method was to revive forms of collective life that had been in abeyance during the Stalin era. This was true of the Communist Party itself, which resumed its practice of holding congresses every two years or so and plenums every six months.

In crude statistical terms, the level of political participation in the USSR was impressive. In 1959, the Soviet Union had 57,000 representative state institutions with 1.8 million deputies. Between 1939 and 1964, 14 million people, or every 10th adult, were elected to the soviets. At election times, around 8 million 'agitators' knocked on doors to expound on the issues of the day and to ensure a decent turnout. By all accounts, their efforts were successful: in one characteristic example, a turnout of 99.98% was reported for the 1975 elections to the Supreme Soviets of the individual republics. And the Soviet Union also scored highly for the social inclusiveness of its grass-roots politics. Of the nearly 1 million deputies elected to local soviets in the RSFSR in March 1961, more than 40% were women and around 60% were workers or collective farm workers. Even this was evidently considered unsatisfactory: by 1975, the proportion of female deputies had climbed to more than 48%.

In addition to reviving these long-standing forms of socialist 'democracy', the regime sought more proactive ways of inducing society to motivate and discipline itself. In 1959, it launched a campaign for popular justice which saw the number of 'comrades' courts' rise from a few hundred to almost 200,000 by the start of 1964. This form of justice was designed to relieve the burden on the judicial system by letting society itself take care of relatively minor offences. The comrades' courts were allowed to require of offenders a public apology or to give them a public reprimand, to impose moderate fines, to recommend sanctions at the workplace, and to demand that offenders made good minor losses incurred by their victims. New regulations of 1963 and 1965 expanded their remit further to include not just drunkenness and hooliganism but also small-scale embezzlement and certain other criminal cases. At the same time, the legal notion of 'hooliganism' expanded to take in a greater range of domestic misdemeanours (including, notably, abusive husbands).

Another method of social control was the creation of 'people's patrols'. By the middle of 1960, 80,000 of these were reported to exist, with a total membership of 2.5 million; by 1965, the numbers had risen to 130,000 and 4.5 million respectively. While the number of active patrollers was surely far lower, the intention was clear. As Khrushchev noted in his speech to a Central Committee plenum in November 1962: 'We have 10 million Party members, 20 million Komsomol members, 66 million members of trade unions. If we could put all these forces into action, if we could use them in the interests of control, then not even a mosquito could pass unnoticed.'

Even without terror, then, the Soviet order remained illiberal. But was it effective? The history of Khrushchev-era legislation suggests that state attempts to police the private domain were more intimidating than effective. The cause of cracking down on good-for-nothings had long been dear to Khrushchev's heart, but although a draft law on social 'parasites' was published in 1957, it met opposition from jurists and was not passed in the RSFSR until May 1961; in 1965, moreover, its remit was narrowed. Coercive measures against the work-shy and the entrepreneurial were becoming more trouble than they were worth for the Soviet system.

In the post-Stalin era, the regime confronted considerable obstacles as it sought to manage society effectively. The population was mobile, and it increasingly moved on its own terms rather than those of the state. Informal economic activity was taking place on a scale that made it ineradicable. The Soviet system also had to cope with the legacy of terror – the millions of people who had suffered punishment and stigmatization under Stalin who were now expected to be contributing members of post-Stalin society. The wave of post-Stalin amnesties was accompanied by a period of (partial) truth and (one-sided) reconciliation.

The return of the formerly excluded and rejected back into the Soviet community brought severe social tensions. These victims of Stalinism did not usually receive a warm welcome, being viewed by their neighbours as spongers or potential criminals. To these social fractures were added the costs of a further wave of urbanization and industrialization. The stresses of the era were most evident in areas of new settlement or recent in-migration, where infrastructure was generally inadequate and social contrasts extreme. The Virgin Lands, for example, were populated not only by bright-eyed Komsomol members but also by local workers, by Gulag inmates and by 'special settlers' (people deported under Stalin as kulaks or members of enemy peoples such as the Germans, Ingush, and Chechens) and their teenage children. The high concentration in an unfamiliar milieu of young men of different backgrounds, the extreme temperatures, the diet of horsemeat, and the availability of vodka brought a succession of pitched battles and other violent incidents. In 1957, hooliganism, assault, and battery together accounted for more than 40% of crimes; about 1.4 million people, moreover, were picked up on the streets for drunkenness. Worse still, from the perspective of Soviet ideology, more than two-thirds of those convicted were workers.

The waning of mobilization

Mass uprisings and public disorder were temporary phenomena attendant on the mass migration and attenuated modernization of the 1950s and 1960s. In the Brezhnev period, such instances of conflict occurred only about once every two years (and they were concentrated in the early years of 1966–8), while under Khrushchev there had been dozens of them. But the decline of protest was not an unmixed blessing for the cause of Soviet socialism. The uprisings of the 1950s and 1960s, to the extent that they had a programme, did not express opposition to the Soviet order. If anything, they were conservative in nature, defending such communist axioms as stable and low prices for basic foodstuffs; and the largest disturbance in a major city came in Tbilisi in March 1956, when an angry crowd in the Georgian capital protested the recent denunciation in Moscow of their most famous son, Joseph Stalin.

The lull of the Brezhnev era represented a stable *modus vivendi* between state and society. Not only did prices remain stable and earning power rise, but social unrest practically ceased (it was instead exported to the Soviet bloc in Eastern Europe, where price rises in the heavily indebted Poland brought people out on the streets in 1970 and 1976). The KGB zealously persecuted the brave but isolated people it considered guilty of 'ideological subversion'. Popular attitudes in Russia were often as conservative as anywhere else in the modern world. A clandestine survey conducted by two Soviet social scientists between September 1968 and March 1969 found that more than three-quarters of a sample of 352 male drillers supported the decision to invade Czechoslovakia. 'My country, right or wrong' was the general position.

The corollary of this, however, was that the kind of constant popular engagement craved by the Soviet regime was not possible. The effects of modernization and the receding prospect of war (at least, the kind of war that would involve large armies and invasions) meant that people could be more self-contained. Large numbers of them were hitting the bottle: by the early 1960s, the average consumption of hard spirits had quadrupled since the 1920s, and in the late 1970s the Soviet Union was afflicted by annual alcohol-related mortality of over 400,000 people. By 1980, the average Soviet person aged 15 or over was consuming almost 15 litres of pure alcohol per year.

Nor was it clear that youthful enthusiasm could any more step into the breach. The success in mobilizing the Komsomol for the Virgin Lands scheme was not repeated under Khrushchev's successors. In 1968, the leadership of this youth organization was handed to a party functionary who, at 40, was comfortably the oldest new incumbent of that post. This was but one symptom of the growing gap between an increasingly apathetic rank-and-file membership, the activists who tried to cajole them, and the functionaries who spoke in their name.

The perestroika era saw an attempt to drag the Soviet population out of its perceived torpor. Mikhail Gorbachev declared he would activate the 'human factor', the latest in a long line of Soviet motivational mantras. Soon, however, reform went beyond slogans to revamp the entire political system. Gorbachev and others within his ruling circle became convinced that the Soviet system must 'democratize' itself. The first multi-candidate elections for local soviets took place in June 1987. A challenge to the political monopoly of the Communist Party was still at this stage unthinkable, but the affairs of that party were becoming more contentious and more public. The 19th Party Conference in 1988 – the first such event for 50 years – was a watershed in Soviet politics. The televised proceedings had the Soviet population glued to its screens. All the while Soviet society was becoming enormously more politically engaged: tens of thousands of 'informal organizations' were springing up, many of them involved to some extent in the burning issues of the day.

In 1989 came the next major development: elections to a new body, the Congress of People's Deputies, which would elect a working parliament. These were still not fully contested elections: candidates were put forward by various organizations, which were thereby guaranteed places in the congress. The Communist Party stuck to the old practice of putting up exactly 100 candidates (including Gorbachev himself) for the 100 places it was allotted. At the end of 1989, democratized legislative bodies were allowed at the level of individual republics, which gave a huge boost to separatist movements. Even more importantly, it provided a basis for political legitimacy in the Russian Republic (RSFSR) that was independent of Gorbachev's power in the Soviet 'centre'. The next two years saw constant conflict between Russian and Soviet institutions and political leaders – a conflict that was resolved in August 1991, when an unsuccessful coup attempt finally discredited the Communist Party of the Soviet Union.

The August events – in which Yeltsin had publicly and telegenically defied the coup leaders and Muscovites had come out in force on to the streets – were instantly mythologized as a moment when popular participation and heroic individuals had come together to bring about epoch-making change. Here was a moment of authentic popular participation to supplant the coup of early November 1917 that had led to the creation of the Soviet Union. But the fact remained that this was no popular rebellion and no Velvet Revolution on Czechoslovak lines. Many Soviet people did not realize they had to choose between the new Russia and the old Soviet Union until the choice had been made for them by the presidents of Russia, Ukraine, and Belarus in December 1991. Perhaps the greatest sign of the Soviet Union's success as a state was that more people did not participate in its downfall.

The fact remained that the period 1987–91 had seen a level of popular engagement remarkable for the citizens of a one-party authoritarian state. At this point, participation finally came out from under the shadow of terror. Meetings were held, newspapers were published and devoured, and society remained at fever pitch as politicians essayed reform and living standards plummeted. In some respects, however, this was a revolutionary conjuncture rather than a great leap into liberal democracy. By the start of the next century, and the arrival of slick televisual 'managed democracy', the new Russia would have neither state violence nor civil engagement, a situation that, while it was greatly preferable to the combination of the two that obtained in Stalin's Russia, still left much to be desired.

Chapter 3
Poverty and wealth

The unrest that brought the fall of tsarism in 1917 started in bread queues. The deprivation endured by a large part of the population of the Russian empire provided the Bolsheviks with much of their political legitimacy. During the Revolution, and for much of the following two decades, to be poor – in theory, at least – was to be politically admirable.

The Soviet Union was a very poor country indeed. It came into being in the midst of a civil war that brought mass starvation: in 1918–22, hunger probably killed more than 10 million people. According to one informed estimate, the only years before 1949 when significant numbers of Soviet people did *not* starve were 1926, 1927, and (with the important exceptions of prisoners and deportees) 1938. Catastrophic peacetime famines occurred in 1921–2, 1932–3, and 1946–7.

The politics of scarcity

Hunger in revolutionary Russia was to a large extent a man-made phenomenon. It grew initially out of the conditions of wartime. The tsarist state had imposed a grain monopoly to maintain a supply of food to the cities and the armed forces. When the Bolsheviks came to power they adopted a more aggressive form of monopoly, instituting in May and June 1918 a 'food dictatorship' of centralized distribution, forced requisition of grain, and the mobilization of rural 'committees of the poor' whose mission was to extract 'surplus' grain from rich peasants, or 'kulaks'.

Like their predecessors in the tsarist wartime administration, the Bolsheviks found that the attempt to gain central control over food supplies brought breakdown in distribution, as peasants retreated into self-sufficient communities and refused to release their grain. The revolutionary regime soon resorted to sheer coercion: it despatched armed detachments to seize grain, created hyperinflation that made barter the main means of exchange, and attempted to set poor peasants against their better-off neighbours. As early as February 1918, Lenin spoke of waging 'ruthless war against the kulaks'.

Already in the early days of the Bolshevik revolution we can see at least three different economic principles at work. The first was a powerful sense of egalitarianism born of historical injustice: the working people had been kept down by landowners and bourgeois who had enriched themselves at the expense of others' toil, and it was now time to right the balance. A decree of 8 November 1917 announced the nationalization of land and granted the peasants use of this resource. While this document made a powerful political statement, in essence it did little more than recognize a situation that had already arisen: peasants had been seizing land and redistributing it among themselves since the middle of 1917.

The second principle was coercive centralization along with hostility to market activity – and even to money itself. The most far-reaching example was the food monopoly, which was unremitting until early 1921. But the centralizing urge also took in non-agricultural sectors of the economy. An All-Russian Council for the National Economy (VSNKh) was set up in December 1917 with a remit to gain control of, and manage, wartime industry. To begin with, nationalization proceeded in piecemeal fashion, its conduct depending heavily on local initiatives, but the policy accelerated in June 1918 with a decree on nationalization of large-scale factories. By October 1919, VSNKh recorded that around 2,500 enterprises, with a workforce of 750,000, had been nationalized; any enterprise that employed hired labour was now considered ripe for state takeover. In combination with the grain requisition measures pursued from mid-1918, these centralizing policies went under the name of 'War Communism'. The organized resource distribution envisaged by some leading Bolsheviks proved unrealistic in wartime conditions of economic collapse, but the experiment of War Communism would form an important precedent for later Soviet thinking on economic planning.

The third principle was that of discriminatory distribution in favour of those groups in society most supportive of, or useful to, the Bolshevik regime. In the Civil War period, the dominant criterion was class. One critical distinction was between 'poor' and 'rich' peasants (though before long the Bolsheviks would refine this by introducing a 'middle' category). The rationing system introduced in the capitals in autumn 1918 was likewise designed according to class principles. In Petrograd, manual workers were entitled to eight times as much as artisans and traders. Class-orientated measures continued throughout the Civil War period.

These three principles sometimes contradicted each other, and in any case were hard to work practically. Coercive state control, as well as creating humanitarian disasters, was often ineffective on the state's own terms. It led to the slaughter of livestock, the concealment of grain, to mass migration and public disorder. During the Civil War, the black market was what kept Russia fed, in as much as it was, and at times even the Bolsheviks had to acquiesce in the shadow economy (for example, by authorizing 'speculators' to bring grain to the city). Under both Lenin and Stalin, periods of aggressive state assault on the economy would alternate with periods of retreat and accommodation. The most famous case occurred in March 1921, when the Bolsheviks, facing popular unrest and collapsing food supplies, gave up their War

Communism for a milder set of measures known as the New Economic Policy (NEP). Draconian requisitioning targets were replaced by a more moderate tax in kind, private trade was legalized within certain limits (many of which were relaxed in due course), and small enterprises were exempted from nationalization. The only major limitation was that large-scale industry and banking remained in state hands. But even large factories were now expected to operate on a commercial footing rather than as branches of a huge and moneyless economic management system.

Another problem was that the Soviet running of the economy quickly became so austere that it alienated even the groups in society who were meant to benefit from revolutionary social justice. Peasants were always likely to do badly from Soviet power, given the Bolsheviks' urban base and long-term commitment to industrialization. But even the ostensibly favoured class of the proletariat had every reason to complain of its lot. After experiments with 'workers' control' in 1917, labour once again became regimented under the principle of 'one-man management'. And the food situation continued to be bleak. A cut in bread rations in January 1921 triggered worker protest that soon spread to the military base on the island of Kronstadt in the Gulf of Finland. The sailors stationed there, hitherto synonymous with revolutionary militancy, issued a set of political demands to the Bolsheviks; although their mutiny was soon suppressed, there could be no clearer evidence that the working-class legitimacy of the Revolution was under threat.

The disastrous provisioning situation of the Civil War was remedied by reducing the burden on the village and allowing peasants to choose what they grew and how much of it they sold. The urban population in the 1920s was fed largely by peasant markets. The problem with this arrangement was that it did not offer a solution to the problem of economic growth – the output of manufactured goods lagged far behind that of agricultural products – and that it left the peasants what the government saw as far too much discretion.

It also left Soviet policy and ideology tying themselves in knots: the emergence of a more affluent peasant sector was both good (in that it demonstrated Russia's advance from a feudal agrarian society to a more developed economy) and bad (since it represented an increase in the numbers of that 'class enemy', the kulaks). In the middle of the 1920s, economic strategy gave rise to fierce debates within the Bolshevik party on the policy to be adopted on the peasantry. The 'left' of the party advocated ending the NEP and exploiting the rural economy to drive forward industrialization and hence proletarianize the still largely agrarian Soviet Russia. The 'right' came out in favour of a more gradualist approach that would advance the economic development of the village in a non-traumatic way but would bring with it the economic stratification that was so hateful to the egalitarian element in Bolshevik thinking. All the while, the definition of a 'kulak' was both elastic and enormously consequential.

War on wealth

The debates were fierce because the issue was thorny. The Soviet Union was a 'backward' country that had undergone a Marxist revolution at an historical moment when, theoretically, it did not qualify. According to Marx's model, intensive economic development and capital concentration would be taken care of by a bourgeoisie of bankers and industrialists. Only when they had done this important historical work would socialists take over. The bourgeoisie would get its hands dirty dealing with all the problems and traumas of economic development: urban squalor, poverty, extreme economic inequality, popular political mobilization, threats of war from similarly industrializing great powers.

Such was the theory, but the reality was that the Bolsheviks in the 1920s were on their own in an agrarian society, surrounded by predatory 'bourgeois' powers, with every incentive to achieve rapid industrial development but with few means to do so. Debates on economic strategy laid bare a fundamental tension in Bolshevik thinking between economic determinism (according to which historical development was subject to 'scientific' laws of economic development) and voluntarism (which recommended radical intervention to speed history up).

The track record of Bolshevism suggested that, at times of stress, the voluntarists were likely to prevail over the determinists, and so it proved again. In the middle of the 1920s, the Soviet government began to rein in the market activity made possible by NEP. Noting that manufactured goods were too expensive for peasants and offered them inadequate incentives to market their grain, it tightened controls over pricing. However, this gave rise to the perennial Soviet problem of shortages, undermined NEP small business, and only accentuated peasant self-sufficiency. At the same time, the idea of long-term economic planning, with priority given to rapid industrialization, was gaining currency and momentum.

Bolshevik economic maximalism came up repeatedly against the intractable peasant question. The anti-market measures of the second half of the 1920s were bound to provoke a defensive reaction from rural producers. As procurement prices fell, so did peasant marketing of grain. State grain collections dipped in autumn 1927. From early 1928 onwards, the Soviet authorities took a series of draconian measures: they closed free markets, persecuted free traders, imposed compulsory grain deliveries on peasants, and resorted to confiscation when the grain was not forthcoming. All the while, anti-kulak rhetoric reached a frenzied intensity unprecedented even in Soviet Russia.

Under Stalin, the Bolshevik Party, now trimmed of its relatively peasant-friendly 'rightist deviation', moved rapidly in the second half of 1929 towards a radical, and by implication violent,

8. Evicting a kulak in Ukraine in 1930

resolution of the peasant problem. Rural areas were to be turned into nothing short of internal colonies to fund the Soviet great leap forward into industrial modernity. The kulaks were to be 'liquidated as a class', and individual peasants were to enter collectives. The results were cataclysmic. Almost two million peasants were exiled to inhospitable parts of Siberia and Kazakhstan in 1930–1 alone. Many others went straight into the rapidly expanding network of concentration camps (later known as the Gulag) that would remain an integral part of Soviet economic strategy until the mid-1950s. Non-kulaks were cajoled or coerced into collective farms.

After a brief slowdown in 1930, the pace of collectivization was merciless: by the middle of 1933, the government claimed that two-thirds of peasant households were in collectives, and by 1936 the figure was close to 90%. But these bare figures give little sense of the *de facto* civil war that collectivization triggered. Faced with the effective confiscation of their property, peasants engaged in desperate resistance – from hoarding of grain to slaughtering of livestock to armed rebellion. The new collectives were chaotic and impoverished, and state procurement targets would have left the peasantry at a low subsistence level at the best of times. These were the worst of times, and the Soviet peasantry was struck by a man-made famine of apocalyptic proportions. Collectivization-related deaths – highest in Ukraine and Kazakhstan – probably came close to six million in 1931–3.

Peasants were always at the very bottom of the Bolsheviks' provisioning hierarchy. Urban people were better supplied, but they did not eat well. By February 1929, grain deliveries had already fallen so far that the whole country was put on bread rationing. The most favoured categories of industrial worker were entitled to 900 grams per day, while the least favoured white-collar workers could count on only a third of that. Rural people, of course, received nothing at all. From the start of 1931, a four-class provisioning system was instituted across the country. At the top of the hierarchy came workers in heavy industry in the capital cities

9. A starvation victim in Kiev, November 1932

and other major centres; at the bottom came white-collar workers. The top two classes made up only 40% of the people on rations, but received almost 80% of supplies.

In the 1930s, hunger and shortages were permanent features of Soviet existence even in the relatively well-provisioned cities. The worst of many bad years was 1933, when the urban population felt the effects of the rural famine caused by collectivization. The abolition of bread rationing at the start of 1935 brought a fall in living standards for many low-income Soviet urbanites, as they were now having to pay higher prices for a major item in their household budget. As late as 1939–40, Soviet people in some cities were having to queue through the night to buy bread. Higher-order commodities were at an even greater premium. When Red Army soldiers invaded eastern Poland in autumn 1939, they found this far from prosperous region to be a consumer goods paradise compared to their homeland. They gorged themselves on local produce and went on a wild spending spree. As a Polish witness noted: 'a hungry world and a satiated world came in contact'.

Visions of plenty

Yet, even in this decade of industrialization and austerity, Soviet thinking was ambivalent about poverty and wealth. Poverty was held to be a defining characteristic of the Russia the Bolsheviks inherited, and a symptom of the hostile and decadent 'bourgeois' order both within tsarist Russia and in the wider world. Morally speaking, it was better to be poor; yet the idea was that poverty was set to disappear under socialism. The Soviet narrative of historical progress included a vision of economic prosperity.

The coming well-being was expressed not only in new factories and industrial output but also in aspects of everyday life. From the 1930s onwards, Soviet media began to put forward visions of a materialistic 'good life'. Frankfurters, ice cream, and caviar were

10. Advertisement for crab meat, 1938

described in loving detail. Anastas Mikoyan, People's Commissar for External and Internal Trade, acquired 22 hamburger machines on a visit to the USA in 1936. The Red October chocolate factory in Moscow produced 500 varieties of confectionery in 1937.

Initiatives extended to goods that by no stretch of the imagination could be construed as proletarian. The new plan of 1937 aimed to raise production of champagne from a few hundred thousand to 20 million bottles per year by 1942.

Was this all for show? Clearly, much of it was. It was easier to produce millions of bottles of champagne than to rectify the urban squalor endured by millions of recent migrants to the city in the 1930s or to give those people a little more to eat. But it is also clear that the Soviet Union even in the 1930s was not immune to the need for modern states to provide material tokens of their legitimacy.

Some Soviet people were able to do better than potatoes and rye bread. The corollary of shortage was privilege. Since the Soviet Union was a distributional state where wealth depended less on money than on access to short-supply goods, the best way to gain access to such goods was to belong to one of the many 'closed distribution' networks in Soviet society. In a category of their own stood the party, government, military, and intellectual elites. The original closed distribution system was the Kremlin, where the revolutionary regime moved from Petrograd in March 1918. The comrades ensconced in this citadel of Russian state power depended entirely on provisioning lists for their food. They lobbied vigorously for their portions (and protested or grumbled when they received less than their due). The Kremlin canteens in the Civil War period were overstretched but still lavishly stocked by the standards of that hungry time: menus featured a wide selection of meat, poultry, fish, vegetables, and even luxury items such as caviar. In the later Soviet period, members of the *nomenklatura* (party-state elite) continued to be well fed. As well as their regular food shopping in limited-access shops, the beneficiaries could take advantage of other perks such as special meals on work trips and congress catering. The elite distribution system grew steadily to the end of the Soviet era. At its peak, just before perestroika, the system of Kremlin food privileges was enjoyed by 8,000 people.

The material well-being of Soviet people would until the very collapse of the USSR depend on their workplace – namely, on the particular closed distribution system that they had at their disposal. In the hungry 1930s and 1940s, this would often be a matter of allotments or farms controlled by an enterprise that would provide its employees with a subsistence minimum. Later on, in the 1960s and 1970s, enterprise directors would establish more elaborate reciprocal relationships with shops, farms, and warehouses, thus slightly alleviating the conditions of the shortage economy for their workers.

Even so, the socialist economy never quite killed the market. The Bolshevik hostility to trade did not prevent the creation of a legitimate private sector of peasant markets and bazaars in the 1930s and 1940s. As late as 1939, white-collar households were buying a third of their potatoes and more than half of their milk and fresh meat in such venues. World War II only accentuated the reliance of Soviet society on the private sector. This was largely, of course, because there was so little of anything to go round. At the end of 1945, more than 80 million people – or about half the population – were getting bread through the centralized rationing system. Conversely, most Soviet people were engaging in barter or frequenting markets in order to survive. In 1943, about 80% of the working-class food budget went on market or other private purchases. And informal economic activity enjoyed a relatively high degree of official acquiescence. Between 1943 and 1946, ration cards were sold more frequently at Russian bazaars than any other class of item.

Such improvised measures did not change the fact that the war made Soviet Russia – both state and individuals – considerably poorer. National income in 1945 was 20% below the pre-war level, and more than 30,000 large industrial enterprises were destroyed or disabled during the war. War losses were equivalent to seven years' worth of economic growth that the Soviet Union would never catch up. Household consumption took a corresponding dip. When, in December 1947, the Soviet Union achieved a propaganda

11. Consumer abundance in *Cossacks of the Kuban*

coup by becoming the first of the combatant nations to abolish
rationing, this led to a short-term worsening of conditions for
urban people, who until then had at least been able to procure
some bread at guaranteed prices. The measure was accompanied
by a currency reform that traded ten old rubles for one new ruble,
thus wiping out savings. As always, however, the peasantry bore
the brunt of Stalinist austerity. The average collective farm worker
in 1945 received only 190 grams of cereals and 70 grams of
potatoes for a day's toil. In 1946–7 came the last great famine of
Soviet history: 1–1.5 million people died as a result of war damage,
harvest failure, and the state's preference to fund reconstruction
rather than keep people alive.

As in the 1930s, mass hunger and hardship were accompanied by
monstrous visions of abundance. The most notorious example was
the collective farm musical *Cossacks of the Kuban*. This feature
film, shot glossily in colour, showed the tables groaning with
produce at a village fair. It was released in 1949 as the real Kuban

The Soviet Union

region was slowly recovering from severe famine. In due course, however, promises of prosperity would begin to gain slightly greater plausibility. Around 1949, the material well-being of the population started to rise from its low base, and there would never be a recurrence of mass hunger. The age of famine had been greatly extended in Russia – about a century further than in Western Europe – but in the last years of the Stalin era it finally ended.

Consumerism and shortage: the post-Stalin era

The Soviet Union was entering a new phase of its existence: basic subsistence was no longer quite such an urgent matter, and consumer welfare was less a matter of myth-making and more a question of practicalities. One of the main political battlegrounds in the power struggle that followed the death of Stalin was the balance to be struck between 'Group A' (heavy-industry) and 'Group B' (light-industry) goods. Nikita Khrushchev, who came out on top, was able at least for a few years to achieve a golden mean: he set about boosting agricultural production, he let the powerful military-industrial complex know that its interests would not be neglected, but he also spoke generally of raising the living standards of the population. By the early 1960s, the regime was tying its legitimacy much more concretely to consumer well-being. Khrushchev made a series of specific promises – notably the pledge to surpass the USA in per capita output of meat, milk, and butter within a few years – that turned out to be politically problematic.

With the mass consumer emphasis, the population's sense of entitlement increased, so that price rises and other austerity measures were likely to arouse protest and even unrest. The unspoken social contract between the Soviet people and its rulers came under greatest strain in 1961–2. First, the regime carried out yet another currency reform. Then it raised prices for basic foodstuffs. The level of protest (known by the Soviet authorities as 'hostile phenomena') in the first half of 1962 was two or three times that of 1961. When the regime sought to shake itself out of the vice of the planned economy, where centralized prices in no way reflected value, it came up hard against notions of social justice that it had itself propagated. Conflict was most acute at the Novocherkassk Electric Locomotive Works in southern Russia, where a strike broke out on 1 June 1962 in response to steep rises in prices for meat and butter that had been announced the previous day. Several thousand troops were deployed, roads were sealed, and telephones cut. The situation soon escalated at a cost of dozens of casualties. This unrest was put down, but Soviet leaders drew the necessary conclusion: never again would they try to raise food prices.

In the Khrushchev era, the Soviet regime's divided attitude to questions of poverty and wealth became positively schizophrenic. On the one hand, the regime remained hostile to market activity, to undue self-enrichment, and to unearned income. The prevailing anti-market egalitarian ethos was also, more positively, reflected in new welfare measures such as a comprehensive pensions law for urban people that was passed in 1956. A further landmark in social policy was a mass housing campaign that saw the construction of more than 35 million new flats between 1955 and 1970 and established the separate dwelling as the right – though not yet always the reality – of every Soviet family. On the other hand, the Soviet system was trapped in the story it insisted on telling of ever increasing prosperity. Among the consequences was a tendency to enter undignified and futile competition with the West over living standards. Hi-tech and diet-conscious America was much less interested than Soviet Russia in claiming supremacy in production of animal fats (even if supremacy was what it continued to enjoy).

After Khrushchev, however, the rhetoric was rather more subdued. For the last 20 years of its existence, the Soviet Union achieved modest but tangible advances on the consumer front. Above all, it maintained its social contract by keeping prices low for the basics. CIA figures (perhaps the best available) estimated a steady growth in food consumption between 1964 and 1973. Between 1946 and 1990, Soviet annual output increased consistently, apart from 1963

12. Shoppers approach Moscow's Central Department Store, the Mecca of Soviet consumerism, 1950s

and 1979 (which were years of bad harvests). Living standards were extremely modest by Western European standards, but until the late 1980s there was no significant downturn, and the Soviet population could enjoy a long period of unprecedented stability. Per capita consumption grew at an average annual rate of 3.5% between 1951 and 1980. The increase in discretionary income was also reflected in levels of savings, which rose from an average of 157 rubles per account in 1960 to 1,189 rubles in 1980.

Another reason that savings increased, however, was that there was very little on which money could be spent. Shortage vitiated the economic upturn that Soviet people enjoyed from the 1960s to the 1980s. This was still a population starved of consumer goods. In 1976, there were only 223 television sets per 1,000 people in the USSR (compared to 571 per 1,000 in the USA). But television production had actually been an investment priority of the Soviet regime. On other consumer fronts it performed even less well. If the Americans had nearly 100 million cars by this time, the Soviet Union could count only 5 million in personal use. In 1970, two-fifths of the average household budget was spent on food.

The continued and systemic failings of distribution were to some extent alleviated by activity in the informal, or 'second', economy. Soviet citizens had always needed to be resourceful to obtain goods and get things done. Some of their activity had been criminal according to Soviet legislation, but much had taken place in various grey areas. By the 1970s, such activity had become a stable and accepted part of Soviet life as never before. In 1965, Khrushchev-era restrictions on cultivation of private plots were lifted. The informal exchange of favours – known in Russian as *blat* – retained disreputable connotations in public but was also recognized by Soviet people as an essential means of getting by under state socialism. Citizens were increasingly able to moonlight, to engage in petty trade, and to make money from services such as hairdressing and car repairs. Even according to official figures, the amount spent by the urban population on privately sold goods rose by 45% between 1975 and 1980. The late Soviet state also had to contend with outright corruption, which ranged from minor theft of state property to thieving on a much larger scale. In 1983, the director of a fruit and vegetables supply organization in Moscow was revealed by investigators to have received hundreds of thousands of rubles in bribes since the early 1970s. Although this was an extreme case, the shortage economy always gave trade workers abundant opportunities to profit from their position.

Another mitigating aspect of state socialism was the Soviet commitment to full employment. In the Stalin period the 'right to labour' proclaimed in the constitution had very often been the right to be conscripted into labour battalions, but by the late Soviet period it often put workers in a position of strength – not for wage bargaining but for exercising discretion in where they worked and how they worked. As much as one-fifth of the industrial workforce, and almost one-third of workers in the construction sector, left their jobs or were fired on disciplinary grounds *each year*. For comparison, labour turnover in the USA in the 1960s and 1970s averaged well below 5% annually. Figures for absenteeism were about twice as high as in America. And the standard work week fell from nearly 48 hours in 1955 to 40.6 hours in 1980.

Towards economic reform

Yet, the consumer stability and relaxed labour discipline of the later Soviet period did not change the regime's core commitment to heavy industry and military spending. At other moments, the Soviet system would have felt more acutely the non-availability of Stalinist methods of coercion, but an economic windfall in the 1970s permitted it to combine welfare and warfare. In October 1973, an oil embargo by a group of Arab countries protesting at Western support for Israel in the Yom Kippur War sent world prices for this commodity spiralling upwards. The Soviet Union, with its vast natural resources, was perfectly placed to profit.

The oil and gas industries, which kept the Soviet economy fuelled in the 1970s and which are so crucial to Russia's fortunes in the early 21st century, are a good illustration of the limitations of the Soviet economic model. The Russian empire had been the pioneer of the world petroleum industry in the 19th century, when oil was struck in the Caucasus (in what is now Azerbaijan). Between the wars, the focus shifted to deposits in the Urals and the Volga basin, but in the 1950s the Soviet leaders realized they were sitting on enormous reserves in Western Siberia. After a strong turn to hydrocarbons in the 1960s, the Soviets could face the oil shock of the 1970s with enormous confidence. But then, the conservatism of the planned economy and the vested interests of regional bosses who wanted to maximize inward investment meant that the Soviet system failed to spot the law of diminishing returns. As existing West Siberian oil reserves passed their peak in the late 1970s, the Brezhnev regime embarked on a crash campaign to save output figures for the five-year plan. The resources poured into production made Soviet oil far more expensive; the result was an enforced, but belated, turn to gas in the early 1980s.

The energy sector was a microcosm (albeit a rather large one) of a command economy where the central planners could not let market mechanisms take over such complex tasks as assessing risk, calibrating supply and demand, and ascribing value. The number of products allocated prices by the planning system was probably in the region of 20 million. Nor did this system make up in transparency and manageability for what it lacked in flexibility. Ever since the first five-year plans, it had led to bottlenecks, hoarding of resources, behind-the-scenes lobbying, and the defence of special interests. By the 1980s, these interests were even harder to dislodge than in the Stalin era, as industrial managers and administrators did not stand to lose their heads for malpractice. For the most part, they were left to run their economic fiefdoms without undue interference as long as, by hook or by crook, they could sign off on plan fulfilment.

This was the economic universe in which Mikhail Gorbachev attempted to intervene. Before he came to power in 1985, Gorbachev had made a career as party boss in his native Stavropol region and then, from the late 1970s, as the leading party authority on agriculture. His past experience of economic management was in the Khrushchevist vein of populist problem-solver. Like Khrushchev, he attempted to unleash popular initiative in order to boost the national economy. The methods he chose were radical enough to undermine the stability of the Soviet order but not radical enough to break free of that order.

By the mid-1980s, the signs of strain in the command economy were impossible for even a Soviet functionary to ignore. Pricing, as so often in the Soviet era, was causing severe distortions in the supply system. As the Minister of Finance reported in April 1987: 'In the stores butter costs 3 rubles 40 kopecks a kilogram, but the cost of its production to the state is 8 rubles 20 kopecks'; beef cost

1.50 to the consumer, 5 to the state. The attempted solutions were designed to give people new incentives. In 1987, state enterprises were placed on a form of cost accounting: managers were now expected to balance their books without bail-outs from the state. In 1988, new legislation on cooperatives brought a reversion to NEP-style encouragement of small business within an overall framework of socialist ownership.

What Soviet people were left with was an unholy combination of state, private, and semi-private economies. Whatever coordination had existed in the command economy seemed to vanish entirely. As economic decentralization was not accompanied by revision of the fixed price system, managers and small business operators had every incentive to hoard resources and to sell goods outside the state system. The new cooperative entrepreneurs had many of the benefits of private ownership without the responsibilities or the risks: after all, the state remained the ultimate owner of their premises and means of production. By 1989–90, the Soviet population was suffering shortages even of basic foodstuffs. The colossal concealed inflation caused by fixed pricing was laid bare on the black market.

What ensued was economic implosion. A population that had got used to steady, if modest, increases in well-being was hit by an alarming short-term dip. It appeared that a would-be modern consumer society had gone back to subsistence. The Soviet order ended as it had started: with food queues. The only difference was that in 1917 the urban population had been clamouring for bread, while in the 1980s sausage entered most discussions of economic reform as the main object of consumer longing and the primary index of a decent life. 'Poverty' and 'wealth' are relative concepts, even if the Soviet regime had stubbornly insisted – with varying results at different times – that they were absolutes. The next step in the history of Russian consumerism – from sausage and rationing to McDonald's and IKEA – would be astonishingly short, and put the late Soviet experience in unforgiving perspective.

Chapter 4
Elite and masses

Back in 1902, Lenin wrote *What Is to Be Done?*, the first ever
Marxist tract on the organization of political parties. From a study
of historical precedent, he concluded that 'the working class
exclusively by its own effort is able to develop only trade-union
consciousness'. In other words, the proletariat might express
particular grievances and protest on particular issues, but on its
own it was unable to mount a concerted challenge to the political
order that kept it down. For that to occur, a disciplined and
organized party of revolutionaries had to assume leadership of the
proletariat.

In summer 1917, when one revolution in Russia had already taken
place and another was in gestation, Lenin stated clearly in his last
major work of political theory, *The State and Revolution*, that the
dictatorship of the proletariat would for the medium term have
more to do with dictatorship than with the proletariat: the
transition from capitalism to communism still required a
'machinery for suppression', namely the state. He did, however,
have a notion of how the masses might, in time, take over this
machinery:

> For when *all* have learned to manage, and independently are
> actually managing by themselves social production, keeping
> accounts, controlling the idlers, the gentlefolk, the swindlers and

similar 'guardians of capitalist traditions', then the escape from this national accounting and control will inevitably become so increasingly difficult, such a rare exception, and will probably be accompanied by such swift and severe punishment . . . that very soon the *necessity* of observing the simple, fundamental rules of everyday social life in common will have become a *habit*.

This vague and evasive projection into the future contrasted starkly with Lenin's cold and pragmatic assessment of present-day political realities. But it shows us one of the main circles that Bolshevik ideology had to square: how was a centralized minority party to claim leadership of the 'masses' in whose name it so often spoke? The Bolsheviks were a tiny vanguard that seized power in an enormous, largely agrarian country. Yet their ideology insisted that a small politically conscious elite could find common cause with the population at large. How was this to be done?

The Bolsheviks and their social base

The Bolsheviks did not necessarily need to be too apologetic. They were a cross between an army and a church, and so could claim obedience and allegiance on grounds other than democratic accountability. Soviet society was effectively at war – whether with internal or external enemies – for the whole of the 1920s and 1930s. It needed authoritative and initiated leadership, not consultation or appeasement. The people needed to be led, and the party had a duty to perform this role. Bolsheviks were proud to be tough and unsentimental. In addition, they had ideological tools to rationalize the unequal relationship between leaders and led. In the Marxist dialectic, the 'consciousness' of the political elite would join with the 'spontaneity' and energy of the masses to impel socialism forward.

Yet, while this model of leadership worked well enough for the Civil War, it was not sufficient in peacetime. The Bolsheviks fretted about their legitimacy, acutely aware of the possibility that thick layers of bureaucracy would come between them and the masses when they set about building a state of their own. The first place they could look for popular credentials was the institution that gave their new country its name. The soviets were redolent of an imagined tradition of direct popular democracy, even if this tradition had more to do with socialist parties other than the Bolsheviks. Under the Bolshevik version of 'Soviet' power, the soviets were soon closely monitored by party agencies.

The crucial institution for adjusting the relationship between elite and masses was the Bolshevik Party itself. Official estimates put party membership at the start of 1917 at only 23,600. Recruitment – especially of the working class – was boosted by the February Revolution and again by the Bolshevik takeover later in 1917. By March 1918, the membership figure given was 390,000. At this point, the Bolsheviks made the first of numerous attempts to tighten up admissions procedures: the result was a fall to 350,000 in March 1919. A 're-registration' campaign of 1919 sought to weed out people who were members in name only: those who did not pay their dues or turn up to meetings, who had quit the Red Army, who had disregarded party instructions, or who had committed 'acts unworthy of a communist'. The result was that party membership fell by 10–15% in urban areas, and much further than that in the villages.

Membership policy would retain this jerky rhythm for much of the Soviet era. The party's role as ideological vanguard had to be combined with its mission to represent, and to incorporate, the 'toiling masses'. As the Soviet equivalent of the church, the party had to maintain doctrinal purity, yet it was also obliged to proselytize and to convert. And the converts were to be not just anybody but people of a distinct class profile: the Bolshevik leadership could not be content if membership growth was driven by white-collar and intelligentsia recruitment at the expense of workers.

On this score, the Civil War era had been a failure. At the time of the tsar's abdication, three in five Bolshevik Party members had been workers, but the proportion had fallen to two in five by the time of the consolidation of Soviet power. Summer 1921 accordingly saw the start of a fresh round of 'purge commissions' where the credentials of 'bourgeois' and white-collar members came under especially close scrutiny. A big boost to the cause of proletarianization then came with the 'Lenin enrolment' of 1924. Within months of the revolutionary leader's death, mass recruitment of workers straight from the factory bench had brought a 40% increase in membership. The next wave came between 1928 and 1931, when hundreds of thousands of new candidate members flooded into the party. By 1932, the Communist (formerly Bolshevik) Party was the most working-class it had ever been. The mass recruitment, however, had done little to assuage Bolshevik anxieties about the ideological rectitude of the membership. Purging and 'verification of party documents' would continue into the 1930s, gradually moving inwards to the centre of power and contributing enormously to the climate of suspicion that made possible the Great Terror. A familiar dynamic was at work: to inject real representatives of the 'masses' into the body of the party undermined that institution's corporate spirit, and periods of mass recruitment were followed by phases of purging.

Beyond the walls of the party, the relationship between elite and masses was even more fraught. Although the Bolshevik revolutionary cause had briefly coincided with peasant priorities in 1917–18, the Soviet regime never did anything more than tolerate the rural population, which it regarded as 'backward' and an obstacle to progress; in due course, it would wage war on the peasantry in the collectivization campaign.

The industrial working class was an entirely different matter: this, in Marxist-Leninist ideology, was the agent of history. Yet the proletariat was not the willing partner in revolutionary change that historical necessity decreed that it should be. It had shrunk drastically during the Civil War period. Moscow had 190,000 industrial workers in 1917 but only 81,000 at the start of 1921. The relationship between party and proletariat came under enormous strain when the former failed to deliver on its revolutionary promises. Food and fuel were in catastrophically short supply. The Bolshevik regime understood the slogan of 'workers' control' very differently from the workers themselves, reimposing centralized management as the norm in 1918 and adopting labour conscription later in the Civil War. In the NEP period, besides long-standing material grievances, workers could complain of desperate overcrowding caused by mass migration to the cities and of unemployment (which exceeded 20% in Moscow in 1927–8). Evidence of working-class grumbling and outright dissent was abundant. As late as 1932, the Soviet leadership was hit by a wave of strikes in the textile industry of the Ivanovo region. For these workers – who included large numbers of women and labour 'veterans' of long standing – class identity still mattered and provided a foundation for collective action against a metropolitan regime that accorded them a far lower priority than the heavy industry workers in Moscow and Leningrad.

Yet there were also signs that the Soviet regime was carrying at least a section of the working class along with it. Real wages grew during the three 'good years' of NEP from 1925 to 1928. Tens of thousands of workers were entering the party, and large factories had a healthy communist presence on the shop floor. Workers were given at least some opportunity to express themselves at production meetings, and what they very often expressed was hostility towards the 'bourgeois specialists' who were still dominant in the technical and managerial positions so crucial to the Soviet Union's transformation into a modern industrialized country. As the next phase of Soviet history would show, such grass-roots resentment could help to fuel state-led crash industrialization.

What ensued between 1928 and 1931 was a phase of radical proletarianization that is usually called 'cultural revolution'.

A large part of it consisted in negative measures: the status and authority of the 'old' intelligentsia were undermined, teachers of 'bourgeois' origins were harassed and dismissed, and a few hundred 'bourgeois specialists' were forced to account for themselves at show trials that were avidly covered in the Soviet press. Conversely, 'proletarian' values and virtues were wildly extolled by writers and broadcasters.

But cultural revolution was not just a matter of symbolic politics. Its more socially tangible results included a massive affirmative action programme that brought hundreds of thousands of workers and their children into higher education and into the expanding technical and managerial occupations. By 1931, 120,000 university students were classified as proletarian, which represented a threefold increase relative to 1928. Over the five years to 1932–3, white-collar representation in higher education fell from just over half of students

13. **Readers crowd a collective farm library in the Kalinin region, mid-1930s. The printed word was widely promoted as the most reliable instrument of self-improvement and self-advancement for Soviet people**

to one-third (even if, given the overall growth of enrolments, there was an increase in absolute terms). Working-class representation increased from one-quarter to a half over the four years to 1931–2.

Hierarchy and egalitarianism: from Stalin to Khrushchev

Here, finally, were signs of the upward mobility that the Revolution was supposed to have made possible. But the immediate political motivation for cultural revolution was less a commitment to social justice than the pressing need to create a new, larger, loyal, and competent elite. In 1927, the party was notably undereducated: under 1% of members had completed higher education, and in many cases this education was not sufficiently technical to fit the demands of the Soviet economy. The engineering and administrative sectors were about to expand enormously in the industrialization drive: the number of civilian engineers rose by a factor of four. The newborn 'proletarian intelligentsia' would fill these jobs.

Cultural revolution was a fleeting window of opportunity for its beneficiaries, not a permanent technique of social engineering. Working-class admissions to higher education dropped back after 1931–2. In the middle of 1931, Stalin himself stepped in to put an end to 'specialist-baiting'. By now, he asserted, the 'wreckers' in industry had been decisively routed, and the remaining members of the old intelligentsia should not automatically be considered untrustworthy. In any case, they would be outnumbered in the new Soviet elite. As Stalin observed: 'No ruling class has managed without its own intelligentsia. There are no grounds for believing that the working class of the USSR can manage without its own industrial and technical intelligentsia.' But this would be a new kind of intelligentsia drawn not only from higher education but also from the factory floor.

Stalin's appropriation of the term 'intelligentsia' was telling. Throughout the 1920s this word had had pejorative connotations of *pince-nez* and privilege, but here it was rehabilitated as a means of talking about the educated elite in a supposedly egalitarian society. In the 1930s, accordingly, the Bolsheviks removed the problem of the non-congruence of party elite and proletariat by toning down their class rhetoric. By 1936, the year of Stalin's constitution, this was declared to be a society beyond class: the antagonistic relationships between social groups due to economic inequities that characterized all other countries and eras had just ceased in the Soviet Union. Soviet society was composed of two full-blown 'classes' (workers and peasants) and one 'stratum' (the intelligentsia).

Sleight of hand with social labels could not on its own remove class antagonism or uneasiness at social inequality in a country with a radically egalitarian ethos. But here Stalinist sociology received abundant assistance from the new mass culture that emerged in the 1930s. Newspapers, films, and broadcasts trumpeted astounding feats of overproduction that served not only to motivate the rest of the workforce but also to legitimate inequality. At the end of August 1935, a miner named Aleksei Stakhanov in the Donbas region of the Ukrainian republic managed to hew 102 tons of coal in a single shift (14 times the norm). Within weeks his achievement gave rise to a nationwide campaign that bore his name. The result was an epidemic of record-breaking workers in all sectors: by December 1935, a list of their feats in heavy industry alone ran to two volumes. While the urge to compete and to streamline production no doubt gave the Stakhanovite movement some of its momentum, the material incentives were also considerable. Mass media coverage dwelled on the rewards that high-achieving workers stood to gain: besides fatter wage packets, they could aspire to such rare consumer goods as bicycles, phonographs, rifles, and wristwatches.

Stalin-era social hierarchy was a matter not merely of possessions but of behaviour. Soviet people in the 1930s were enjoined to become 'cultured', which meant not only the reading of books and

14. A view of Gorky Park in the mid-1930s. This park was a showcase for 'cultured' leisure in the Stalin era

the imbibing of approved Soviet knowledge but also the adoption of the appropriate lifestyle. Curtains, lampshades, and tablecloths were now *de rigueur* for the civilized Soviet household – even if that was only a partitioned corner of a room. Fashionable clothes, cosmetics, and perfumes became publicly respectable, even desirable, in the second half of the 1930s. On a more prosaic level, the norms of 'culturedness' required the Soviet person to be clean and well groomed and to change his or her underwear regularly. This mixed bag of lifestyle recommendations constituted a package of what in other countries would have been called 'middle-class values'. It had little in common with the proletarian austerity of earlier phases of Soviet history.

The interlude between Great Terror and war confirmed that egalitarianism was much less important to the Soviet regime than effective mobilization. In October 1940, the Soviet government brought in fees for higher education, specialized technical schools, and the last three years of ordinary secondary schools. This was a war economy measure to release more young people for vocational training and to correct an imbalance in the labour force caused by expansion of higher education. But the effect was to accentuate certain social differences: this was a period when the upper levels of the intelligentsia were extremely well rewarded relative to the rest of the workforce.

But the war also saw a great dilution of the Soviet Union's key feeder institution for the elite: the Communist Party. The years 1941–4 returned to – even surpassed – the most indiscriminate recruitment policies of the early revolutionary period. Men were accepted into the party in their droves straight from their army units. By December 1943, 56% of party members were in the armed forces (as compared to 15% at the time of the German invasion in June 1941). And this recruitment was more 'democratic' than hitherto: almost a third of wartime admissions were classified as workers, and just over a quarter as peasants. To an unprecedented degree, ordinary men (and women: 800,000 of them served at the front during the war) might feel they had a stake in their country's dominant political organization. By the second year of the war, the right to define what made a good party man lay more with the fighters at the front than with the ideologues in the rear. Here, despite ruthless military discipline that brought the execution of more than 150,000 Red Army soldiers, was the closest that the interests of the state and the population came to converging in the Soviet era.

The mass wartime recruitment posed a familiar problem for the Soviet leadership in peacetime: how was the party to retain its identity as a disciplined upholder of ideological orthodoxy when it was full of so many new arrivals with such a sense of empowerment and entitlement? In January 1946, only one-third of members had been in the party before June 1941. The response was a shift back to a more restrictive admissions policy. In some areas of the Soviet Union, admissions practically ground to a halt in the late 1940s, which led to an absolute fall in party membership in 1948 and 1949.

The conservatism of admissions policy was matched by a reaffirmation of Stalinist culturedness. Soviet films produced during and just after the war contain an impressive number of well-appointed bourgeois households tended by women whose commitment to the domestic front (with a few dastardly exceptions) is impeccable. A famous study by Vera Dunham of the 'middlebrow' Soviet fiction of the late 1940s revealed the extent to which tablecloths and elegant crockery were a social norm conveyed by socialist realist writing in this period. Dunham identified what she dubbed a 'Big Deal' between the regime and an emerging 'middle class' of party functionaries, valued specialists, and industrial managers. Even if it is legitimate to wonder how many members of Soviet society, whatever their value to the regime, enjoyed the comforts described in these novels, this neat phrase captures a basic truth of mid-century Soviet civilization: the Soviet order had stabilized, it had a reasonably secure elite, and this elite was feeling entitled to its share of material rewards.

Yet this remained an uncomfortable state of affairs for a regime with a notional commitment to egalitarianism and an enduring anti-intellectual bias. The next Soviet ruler, Nikita Khrushchev, sought to reinvigorate the forms of mass democracy that had ossified under Stalin. Once again the doors of the party were flung open. The 1950s saw a recruitment drive whose beneficiaries (unlike those of 1941) were likely to stay alive for a while. Between 1956 and 1964, new enrolments increased every year except 1960. By mid-1965, party membership topped 12 million – an increase of 70% since Stalin's death. The Khrushchev recruitment drive was also underpinned by a 'democratic' rationale: between 1956 and 1961, 40% of new arrivals in the party were workers at the time they joined, and more than 20% were collective farm workers. Complementary policies included a shift back to equalization in wage policy and a short-lived attempt to make vocational training mandatory for school-age adolescents. Khrushchev also weighted university admissions in favour of working-class applicants: priority was given to candidates who came with a

Рисунок К. ЕЛИСЕЕВА.

— Согласны ли вы поехать на периферию!

ХОР РОДСТВЕННИКОВ: — Н-е-е-е-т!!!

15. In this Soviet satirical cartoon of 1956, a young man (with a suitably foppish haircut) is asked at a work placement commission: 'Are you willing to move to the periphery?' (in other words, to the back of beyond). A 'chorus of relatives' intervenes on his behalf

recommendation from their employer. By the end of the Khrushchev era, almost two-thirds of students in higher education had work experience.

Inequalities were further reduced by a series of welfare measures. A new minimum wage narrowed the gap between white- and blue-collar work. Through a mass housing campaign the Khrushchev government proclaimed its ambition to ensure equality of outcomes in this most fraught of social policy areas. Besides staggering rises in output, the aim was to simplify the complicated existing system – according to which different organizations and institutions had control of their own housing stock – and create more transparent municipal housing queues. In Moscow, for example, almost 200,000 families were enrolled on the queues by January 1964 (as compared with 40,000 at the end of the Stalin era). While the system did not work entirely as it should have done, and remained vulnerable to special interests and to abuse, this was a powerful gesture towards egalitarianism.

Of course, the contradiction between the existence of an enclosed elite and the rhetoric of mass democracy did not lessen. The gap between the *nomenklatura* and everyone else remained palpable. If anything, it widened, as the removal of terror meant that functionaries did not need to worry about losing their life, their position, or their privileged access to special grocery stores and holiday resorts. Conversely, peasants were still third-class citizens; their freedom of movement remained drastically curtailed until 1974, when a new statute at last stipulated the issuing of passports to collective farm workers.

Modernization and social change

In the post-Stalin decades, existing hierarchies were challenged and redefined less by specific government initiatives than by long-term demographic and social developments. The 'masses' were not what they had been earlier in the Soviet period. In the early 1960s, the balance between rural and urban populations in the USSR finally tipped towards the latter, and the momentum of migration did not diminish in the following decade. The best part of 25 million people moved to the cities between 1939 and 1959, and the rural population continued to plummet thereafter. Migration out of the village totalled almost 20 million in the RSFSR alone between 1961 and 1980.

Even before he became Soviet leader, Khrushchev had signalled his intention to devise a policy on the village to replace the coercion and malign neglect of the Stalin period. From 1953 onwards, he was in a position to put intention into practice, reducing the tax burden on the peasantry and channelling more resources into the rural economy. But the post-Stalin state vision of the village remained profoundly coercive. The plan was to urbanize the village, to streamline agricultural production, and to let fewer productive communities die out. In the 1950s, only 120,000 of the 700,000 villages in the USSR were considered viable by the authorities. Here, in a sense, was the apotheosis of the Soviet modernizing mission: the collectivization of the 1930s had bludgeoned the peasantry into submission, but now rural people were to become productive modern citizens. For those rural people who were not condemned to live out their lives in 'dying' villages, life chances became preferable to those of the Stalin era. In the late 1930s, more than half of rural people aged 15 to 25 had spent less than 5 years in school; by the late 1950s, that figure had fallen well below 10%.

The Soviet Union, which had always claimed to be a country for the 'masses', was now acquiring a modern 'mass society': a predominantly urban civilization with an almost universally accessible, primarily audiovisual, mass culture. The task of 'radiofication' was deemed complete by 1960, while television could be called a truly national medium by 1970. The number of television sets in the Soviet Union went up from 5 million to 25 million over the course of the 1960s, while the number of stations rose from 9 in 1955 to 121 in 1965. As for audience response, the evidence suggested that Soviet viewers were no more inclined than their Western counterparts to use the new medium for self-improving purposes. High levels of television watching correlated neatly with low levels of education. Television provoked the same fears – social atomization, lobotomization – as elsewhere in the modern world, and such cultural anxiety had additional bite in a country notionally committed to 'rational' or 'active' leisure. None of this, however, could change the fact that viewing figures were rising steadily for all sections of society in the 1970s.

Demographic indicators also pointed in the direction of modernity and individualization. Soviet people were now marrying later, having fewer children, and divorcing more readily. The proportion of women in the RSFSR marrying before the age of 20 fell from 29% in 1926 to 19% in 1970. The average Soviet family contained 2.8 children in 1959 but only 2.4 in 1970 (though figures varied substantially between republics and between urban and rural populations). The divorce rate shot up after legislation was liberalized in 1965. Within a few years it was around 3.5 per 1,000 (or more than three times the rate in 1940). Yet, in a dismaying reminder of the limits of modernization in Soviet society, a high divorce rate and widespread tolerance of early sexual activity did not bring in their wake adoption of modern contraceptives. Soviet women were suspicious of the Pill because of its supposed carcinogenic properties, and the authorities, gripped by fears of demographic crisis, did everything they could to encourage such beliefs. Abortion remained a primary method of birth control right to the end of the Soviet period. Official statistics even in the late 1980s gave a figure of six to seven million induced abortions per year – about one-fifth of the total for the entire world.

Soviet-style modernization did not just mean homogenization and television-watching anomie. It also brought changes to the elites of Soviet society. The rising educational standards of Soviet society made professional training a prerequisite for career advancement. This process was evident even in the village. In 1965, two-thirds of collective farm chairmen were agricultural specialists; by 1982, the figure had risen to almost 97%. More generally, the Soviet professional middle class grew to unprecedented dimensions. As befitted a middle-aged country, the Soviet Union thickened around the middle. The intelligentsia 'stratum' swelled with the expansion of tertiary education in the post-Stalin era. By the end of the 1960s, more than six million people with higher education were employed in the Soviet economy. By the end of the Soviet era, that figure was close to 15 million. Educated 'specialists' constituted 10% of the Soviet population in the early 1960s, but around 20% by the start of the 1980s.

The average level of education of white-collar employees grew substantially. If in 1941 only about one in five employees had higher or specialized technical education, by 1960 the figure was about 50%, and by the late Soviet period close to 100%. In 1956, more than two-thirds of factory directors had learned their trade on the job, but already in the mid-1960s the clear trend was for formal training. And the trend was only confirmed when Khrushchev's experiments with class-based admissions to higher education were scaled down in 1965.

The life and values of the 40-million-strong 'mass intelligentsia' dominated Soviet society and culture. Heroic feats of exploration or construction belonged to an earlier era of socialist realism. Now writers and film-makers turned increasingly to everyday life, with its unheroic equivocations and comic mishaps and misunderstandings. In the cinema of the time, it was hard to come by plausible depictions of the working class or (still less) the peasantry. The lines of social hierarchy were clearly drawn, and status was by now strongly hereditary. A decent higher education – the main passport to success later on – was close to guaranteed to the children of parents who had themselves had such an education. Tertiary education and appropriate white-collar employment was the aspiration for this society that claimed to respect manual labour like few others.

Against this social backdrop there could be no return – even rhetorical – to the egalitarian experiments of earlier in Soviet history. What this implied for the long-term viability of the Soviet system was unclear. In a famous 1969 essay 'Will the Soviet Union Survive Until 1984?', the dissident Andrei Amalrik identified the emergence of a Soviet middle class, a kind of communist bourgeoisie. At the same time, he argued, the ruling regime was becoming more and more isolated and concerned with its own self-preservation rather than any long-term ideological goal. Amalrik surmised that a lot would depend on the way that the party elite found an accommodation with the middle class: would it make timely concessions, or would it jealously guard its privileges and provoke the kind of conflict that occurred in France in 1789 after the convocation of the Estates General or in Russia in the early 20th century? Amalrik saw few grounds to expect far-sightedness from the Communist Party, though he did mention the possibility that the middle layer of the Soviet social 'sandwich' might expand so far as to disable unrest from below and obstruction from above.

In the event, it was the elite itself that precipitated the fall of the Soviet Union, and it did so by attempting to rouse the 'masses' to action once again: to drag society out of its late industrial rut. By the 1980s, two decades of stable urban existence had dampened the traditional 'campaigning' fervour of the Soviet order. By now, mass culture extolled not feats of productivity and acts of self-sacrifice for the common good, but the grey areas of everyday life and emotional problems. Soviet society was not a lumpy monolith to be chivvied into motion but rather a compound of variously self-interested individuals and groups. Thus, when Gorbachev unleashed on the Soviet Union partially free elections and limited forms of free enterprise, the results were troubling. The masses stubbornly refused to act with a single mind.

More disastrous for the future of the Soviet Union was the fact that the elite itself was now more diverse and unruly than at any previous moment in Soviet history. The one-party system had reproduced itself stably since the 1960s, but the price it paid for the absence of terror was internal incoherence. It contained not one party but – in embryonic form – several. Party members ranged from social democrat *manqués* to Stalinist statists, from regionalists and nationalists to internationalists. By 1991, the differences between them would drain the legitimacy and the power from the Soviet system.

In this light, the quickly mythologized events of August 1991 – when protesters in Moscow famously defied the tanks sent out by the coup leaders – were more a distraction than an indication of the real causes of the Soviet collapse. The crucial factor was the inability of the plotters to mobilize their own elite. Once again, to adopt a famous dictum of Stalin, cadres had decided everything – but this time the Soviet Union had neither the carrots nor the sticks to keep them loyal.

Chapter 5
Patriotism and multinationalism

The Soviet Union was built on a paradox: here was a major power, created at an historical moment when empires were falling apart and the nation-state was recognized as the natural form of political existence, that claimed to be multinational in its internal affairs. The Soviet state recognized the existence on its enormous land mass of more than a hundred 'nations and nationalities'. At the end of the Soviet period, 22 of these could claim populations on Soviet territory of more than one million. Yet, as part of its grand historical mission, the USSR had set out to achieve a sense of commonality that could not only hold together dozens of distinct ethno-national groups but transcend nationalism altogether.

Not only did nationality carry weight in the administrative structure of the USSR, it mattered to ordinary people too. Western visitors to Soviet Russia could expect to be quizzed by acquaintances on their own nationality, and answers such as 'American' or 'British' were considered unsatisfactory. These were administrative, or at best civic, nationalities, but Soviet people were interested in ethnic identities: they wanted to find out whether people were Irish, Spanish, or Polish because, in their own society, they needed to identify fellow citizens as Tatar, Ukrainian, Jewish, and so on. Knowledge of a person's ethnic origins allowed Soviet people to make judgements about their trustworthiness, work capacity, and temperament. Soviet ethnic humour had no end of butts and protagonists: crafty Jews, Georgian spivs, clever Armenians, dozy Ukrainians, and imbecilic Chukchi (an indigenous people from north-eastern Siberia).

This everyday salience of nationality was due not only to time-honoured ethnic prejudice but also to government policy. The machinery of the state served people constant reminders that they had sub-Soviet identities and allegiances. The crucial identity document in Soviet society, the internal passport, had a separate clause for nationality: each citizen was required to specify this at the age of 16 (choosing the nationality of his or her parents, or the nationality of one of them in the case of an ethnically mixed marriage). In this way, the system turned nationality into a permanent and inherent characteristic of each Soviet person. Yet at the same time, unofficially, some people were able to select a nationality that had not come down to them by family inheritance (most often the assumed nationality was Russian, for example in the case of some Soviet Jews who wished to avoid discrimination). People also had opportunities to develop allegiances that might not correspond to their passport nationality: if a citizen was classified as Ukrainian at age 16, she might subsequently reside in the Belorussian republic, speak Russian, marry a Tatar, yet identify herself in the census as Jewish.

The prominence of nationality as a category is unexpected in a state that, in its early days especially, espoused a class-based theory of historical progress. What are we to make of this? Was the recognition by the Soviet state of national cultures and territories merely an act of deception that concealed centralizing or Russifying designs? Was the Soviet Union an empire under another name? A review of the titles of important recent books on Soviet nationalities reveals much uncertainty on this point: their authors describe the USSR variously as a 'state of nations', an 'affirmative action empire', and an 'empire of nations'.

Nationality in early Soviet practice

Historians are uncertain in large part because the Bolsheviks themselves were unsure of what to do about nationalism. As the centre of gravity of revolutionary Marxism shifted from Western to Eastern Europe in the late 19th and early 20th centuries, the national question became ever harder to ignore. Socialists had their best chance of making a political impact in the ethnically variegated empires of Eastern Europe: the Austro-Hungarian and the Russian.

Karl Marx's attention had largely been focused on more ethnically homogeneous states. His writings gave few answers to a question that was coming to preoccupy the Russian revolutionary movement: what was Marxism to do about nationalism? Opinions among Marx's successors differed. At one extreme lay a steadfast commitment to proletarian internationalism that left no space for ethnic or territorial particularity. At the other lay a belief in the right of national groups to self-determination. Somewhere in between came federalism and an 'extra-territorial' model of cultural autonomy for minority national groups within a unitary state.

The incipient disintegration of the Austro-Hungarian and Russian empires in World War I concentrated Marxist minds still further. Lenin began advocating a policy of 'self-determination' shortly before the war, and this phrase became the key to nationality policy after the October Revolution. His stance owed a good deal to pragmatism: there was little point in antagonizing national groups whose actions the Bolsheviks were powerless to control in late 1917 or 1918.

The remarkable fact, however, was that proclamations of self-determination did not prevent the Bolsheviks from setting up a new state, the Soviet Union, that at the time of its founding in 1922 included most of the territory of the old Russian empire. Only the more developed westernmost nations – Poland, Finland, and the Baltic states – had managed to stay firmly out of the union. How did this reincorporation occur?

One obvious answer is that the Bolsheviks used violence and subversion. The most flagrant example came in Georgia, which had a stronger indigenous (non-Bolshevik) socialist movement than any other successor state to the Russian empire. But this small country in Transcaucasia was granted little more than three years of independent existence before the Red Army chased out the incumbent Georgian Mensheviks in February 1921. In the less stable neighbouring states of Armenia and Azerbaijan, the Bolsheviks also took a firm hand, though in these cases it is less obvious that their takeover was usurpation. Estonia, Latvia, Lithuania, and Finland were established as independent states not because Russia's new regime magnanimously allowed them to go their own way but because they beat off the Bolshevik challenge (with a little help from the Germans).

But to view the Bolshevik slogan of self-determination as a Machiavellian plan to reconstitute the Russian empire under a different name is too simple. This phrase did not provide much in the way of practical guidance. The disintegrating Russian empire contained numerous national or proto-national groups, and it was unclear how they would react to the revolutionary situation. The most complex situation arose in Ukraine, where power changed hands dozens of times between Reds, Whites, and Ukrainian nationalists. In many cases, the 'nations' in question did not want independence or could not even conceive of it. In Central Asia there was little sense of which nations might exist to exercise their right of self-determination.

During the Civil War, Bolshevik policy was very often guided by the exigencies of combat: the Soviets were obliged to take allies where they could find them, even if that meant doing business with national elites who were anything but Bolshevik. But this was also a time when a new orthodoxy – developed by Lenin and by his Commissar for Nationalities, Joseph Stalin – took shape.

Stalin's main task was to find a third way between the extreme antipathy to national sentiment that was felt by many of his Bolshevik comrades and the 'softer' versions of federalism (which would allow the nations far more autonomy than state-building revolutionaries could tolerate). His solution to this conundrum was to make the existence of a homeland territory central to his definition of a 'nation'. If enough members of a given nationality were concentrated on a particular territory, they should be granted nationhood in administrative terms. In due course, this would lead to the formation of a 'union' whose dozen members themselves contained additional 'national' units. The most complex structure was to be found in the Russian Republic (RSFSR), whose federal structure by the mid-1920s contained 20 nationally defined 'autonomous republics' and 'autonomous regions' from Crimea to Yakutia.

Lenin and Stalin's relatively pluralist position on nationalities met fierce opposition from other members of the party. It was also received with hostility by Russian or Russified Bolsheviks in the regions, who were dismayed that the centre seemed to be favouring local particularism over political reliability. But Lenin insisted that the non-Russian nationalities must not be needlessly antagonized, going so far as to exclude the word 'Russian' from the name of the new state that was created in 1922.

The creation of national territories went along with the encouragement of many of the key attributes of nationhood: teaching and publishing in the national languages, training up and promoting indigenous elites, and fostering national cultures. The Bolsheviks, in other words, were willing to encourage nation-building in all ways that did not involve political autonomy.

This set of policies – which went under the general name of 'indigenization' (*korenizatsiia*) – took shape during the Civil War

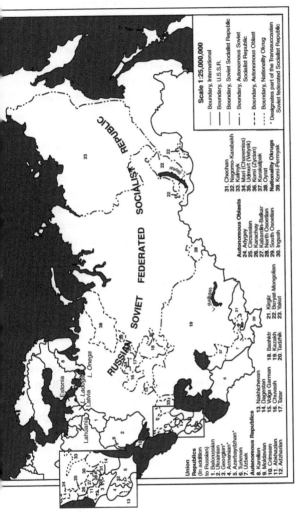

Map 1. This map presents a snapshot of the ethno-territorial boundaries in the Soviet Union. By the late 1930s, the total number of national units had risen from 39 to 51, and 3 more territories (the Tajik, the Kyrgz, and the Kazakh) had been raised from the status of 'autonomous republic' to that of 'union republic'

Scale 1:25,000,000

——— Boundary, International
——— Boundary, U.S.S.R.
——— Boundary, Soviet Socialist Republic
– – – Boundary, Autonomous Soviet Socialist Republic
— · — Boundary, Autonomous Oblast
· · · · · Boundary, Nationality Okrug

* Designates part of the Transcaucasian Soviet federated Socialist Republic

Union Republics
(In addition to Russian)
1. Beloussian
2. Ukrainian
3. Georgian*
4. Armenian*
5. Azerbaydzhan*
6. Turkmen
7. Uzbek

Autonomous Republics
8. Karelian
9. Moldavian
10. Crimean
11. Abkhazian
12. Adzhezian
13. Nakhichevan
14. Daghestan
15. Volga Garman
16. Chuvash
17. Tatar
18. Bashkir
19. Kazakh
20. Tadzhik
21. Kirgiz
22. Buryat-Mongolian
23. Yakut

Autonomous Oblasts
24. Adygey
25. Circassian
26. Karachay
27. Kabardin-Balkar
28. North Ossetian
29. South Ossetian
30. Ingush
31. Chechen
32. Nagorno-Karabakh
33. Kalmyk
34. Mari (Charemiss)
35. Udmurt (Vetyak)
36. Komi (Zyrian)
37. Karakalpak
38. Oyrat

Nationality Okrugs
39. Komi-Permyak

RUSSIAN SOVIET FEDERATED SOCIALIST REPUBLIC

L. Ladoga
L. Onega
Lahuanga
Latvia
Estonia
Balkaş
Darian

and was pursued systematically in the 1920s. It led to the creation of thousands of 'national' soviets at lower levels of the administrative pyramid. The Bolsheviks were 'internationalist nationalists' who were building the world's first ever 'affirmative action empire': they were systematically promoting the backward and underprivileged nationalities, yet they also operated according to a strict hierarchy between the centre and the periphery (the new name for the old imperial opposition between metropole and colonies).

Indigenization was not just a practical expedient for the running of a multi-ethnic state. Nor was it primarily a sop to nationalist aspirations: in many cases, the Bolsheviks had a stronger sense of the nations to which people should belong than the people did themselves. Rather, the policy of encouraging nationhood was based on a Marxist view of historical progress according to which 'backward' nations would advance to socialism. According to this interpretation, nationhood was an inescapable side-effect of modernization; without experiencing it, the variegated ethnic groups of the former Russian empire had no hope of reaching the historical goal marked out by the Bolsheviks.

The Bolsheviks took this project very seriously in the 1920s. They used nationality as a far-reaching principle of territorial organization. They worked in combination with ethnographers to determine how many nations did in fact exist in the USSR. In some cases, they created nations with multi-million populations from nothing. In 1924, for example, the Soviet Union brought into being a new nation, Turkmenistan, in a part of what had formerly been the tsarist colony of Turkestan. The newly minted Turkmen had little sense of what united them, given the salience of sub-ethnic sources of identity such as tribe and ancestry. But the local elite seized on the gift of nationhood, and the opportunities of indigenization, with some alacrity, feeding off resentment at other Central Asian groups and at the Russians themselves.

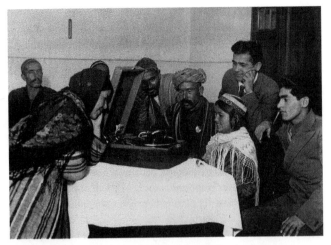

16. **Tajik collective farm workers listening to the gramophone, Moscow 1935: a typical demonstration of the Soviet 'friendship of peoples'**

Patriotism and ethnic cleansing

In the late 1920s, however, the Soviet regime, without ever renouncing indigenization entirely, took several steps back from it. Having invested great effort in presenting the veil as a national symbol in Uzbekistan in the 1920s, the Bolsheviks in 1927 began a campaign against it. Those regional elites who had indigenized too wholeheartedly were now branded 'bourgeois nationalists' and stood to lose their jobs and much else besides when the party began to purge itself. The policies of indigenization, which had often pitted one ethnic group against another in small localities, left a bitter residue of resentment and antagonism.

In the early 1930s, as the tension between indigenization and state-building increased, the Bolsheviks began to work intensively on creating a unitary Soviet patriotism. Moving away from the excessively abstract revolutionary doctrine of proletarian internationalism, they developed instead a more populist, state-centred Soviet identity which had a strong Russian colouration. By 1937 – the centenary of the death of Aleksandr Pushkin, now reclaimed as a progressive political hero – the Bolshevik Revolution was firmly established as the culmination of a triumphalist timeline: as well as being revolutionaries, the Bolsheviks were also heirs to a great tradition of Russian great power status and high culture. The primacy of the Russians in Soviet society at this time is confirmed by the readiness with which others were joining their ranks. One good estimate holds that Russification (the adoption of Russian identity by non-Russians, usually as a result of migration or intermarriage) was responsible for nearly half of the increase in the ethnically Russian population between 1926 and 1939.

The policies of the 1930s were not just a matter of building up a new sense of Soviet identity: they also went hand in hand with a decade or more of state-sponsored violence on ethnic principles. The drift to terror started in Ukraine, a sensitive border region where the Bolsheviks feared disloyalty in the event of the European war for which they were always bracing themselves. A show trial of Ukrainian nationalists in March–April 1930 served notice of Moscow's mixed feelings about Ukrainization. The central party's outright rejection of the self-assertive indigenization pursued in this republic was clinched at the end of 1932, when Politburo decrees pinned the blame for catastrophic failures of grain requisitioning on excessive Ukrainization. The ensuing year-long terror campaign destroyed local communists sympathetic to indigenization as well as more predictable targets such as Ukrainian nationalist intellectuals and western Ukrainians who had emigrated from Poland to the Soviet Union in the 1920s.

Events in Ukraine were an early sign of a shift to ethnically based repression in the 1930s. One of the legacies of indigenization was primordialism: the sense that nations were not recent political constructs but rather had deep roots in a particular homeland, language, and culture. In the 1920s, this had meant that dozens of

Soviet 'nations' deserved administrative recognition. In the 1930s and 1940s, it might mean that they deserved mass arrest and deportation. Between the mid-1930s and the early 1950s, the USSR saw wave after wave of ethnically based repression. The first victims of Soviet ethnic cleansing, in 1935–6, were Germans, Poles, and Finns in the western border regions, and Estonians, Latvians, and Finns in the Leningrad region. In 1937–8, the range of nationalities targeted for repression extended to the Far East. More than 170,000 Koreans were deported to Kazakhstan and Uzbekistan, and a few thousand Kurds and Iranians were forcibly removed from territory adjoining Iran and Afghanistan. Repression then spread inwards from the border regions: during the Great Terror of 1937–8, almost a quarter of a million people were executed as part of 'national operations' (mass arrests targeted at particular national groups). The war saw a further wave of ethnic deportations. Between July and October 1941, hundreds of thousands of Soviet Germans were removed from their homes in Ukraine and European Russia to exile in Western Siberia and Kazakhstan. In 1943–4, a number of peoples allegedly guilty of collaboration with the Germans were given similar treatment: the Karachai, Balkars, Chechens, and Ingush in the Caucasus, the Kalmyks in the western steppe, and the Crimean Tatars. In all cases, conditions of deportation and resettlement were such as to guarantee high mortality: about one in five of the Crimean Tatars deported to Uzbekistan were dead by the end of 1945.

The later 1940s saw campaigns against partisan resistance in Ukraine and the Baltic republics, deportations of tens of thousands of Estonians, Latvians, and Lithuanians, and crackdowns against perceived manifestations of nationalism in locations from Armenia to Buryatia. This was also a period when the Jewish population became a new target of organized state repression. The rise in the self-awareness of Soviet Jews as a consequence of the Nazi genocide, and their enthusiastic response to the creation of the State of Israel in 1948, made them both a perceived fifth column and an unwelcome challenge to the Russo-Soviet cultural orthodoxy of mature Stalinism. The response was a crackdown on education, publishing, and other cultural expression in Yiddish, along with anti-Semitic purges in the party-state apparatus, the professions, and the arts and media. The campaign ended the careers – and in some cases the lives – of many prominent Soviet people; without Stalin's death in March 1953, it might have gone as far as mass repression.

Following its victory in World War II, the Soviet Union was left with a hypertrophied version of the populist patriotism launched in the 1930s. By now the Russians were not only first among equals in the fraternal ethnic community of the USSR; they also led the world in all worthwhile fields of endeavour. They had invented radio, the aeroplane, the light bulb – perhaps even football.

Yet, during the Stalin period, Russification remained a prominent side-effect of the campaign to build Soviet patriotism rather than a goal in itself. Even at the height of the campaign against 'bourgeois nationalism' in 1938, the USSR failed to pass a law that would give non-Russians the right to have their children educated in Russian. Right up to 1959, in the mid-Khrushchev era, members of the titular nationality of a given republic were – on paper, at least – required to receive schooling in their native language.

The USSR also retained its ethno-federal structure. The thousands of national soviets that had sprung up in the 1920s had been abolished in 1936, but the basic national-territorial structure had remained, even if it now had far fewer units. The proponents of indigenization had been terrorized in the 1930s, but the policy itself had never been renounced, and many of its administrative underpinnings were still in place.

Nationalities after Stalin

These factors became more politically meaningful in 1953, soon after Stalin's death, when the Soviet state retreated decisively from ethnic violence. Five of the eight 'traitor peoples' deported during the war were rehabilitated in 1956-7 and permitted, at least in principle, to leave their place of exile. Nikita Khrushchev, the new leader who emerged from the power struggles following Stalin's death, dealt several large favours to the Ukrainians; not least, he transferred to them the Crimea in 1954 (even if this gesture was largely a means of consolidating the Slavic hold over the peninsula following the deportation of the Tatars during the war).

Yet it soon became obvious that the original goal of Soviet nationality policy – to create the conditions for the 'backward' nationalities to catch up their more developed counterparts and ultimately to transcend nationalism – was remaining elusive. From the 1960s onwards, Soviet leaders acknowledged in their rhetoric that nations were here to stay: they spoke vaguely of 'rapprochement' rather than the 'fusion' of national groups that had earlier been an axiom of Soviet ideology. The objective was now to manage nationalism rather than to overcome it.

But even this was a difficult task. By the 1970s and 1980s, it was clear that an early Bolshevik assumption – that modernization would lead to the erosion of national sentiment – had been mistaken. In the postwar era, urbanization tended to make members of the indigenous nationality migrate to the cities of their own republic. Between 1959 and 1989, the cities of all union republics apart from Estonia and Latvia became to a significant degree 'de-Russified'; by 1989, members of the indigenous nationality predominated in the cities of all republics other than the Kazakh and the Kyrgyz. Soviet cities were not becoming multinational melting pots where citizens lost touch with their original ethnicity. People were showing clear signs of emotional attachment to a particular 'homeland' within the socialist union.

Another reason for rising national consciousness was the fact that non-Russian national groups were acquiring larger educated elites. Georgians, for example, made up only two-thirds of their republic's population in 1970, but their representation in higher education there was well over 80%. Between 1979 and 1985, all 14 non-Russian republics improved their levels of educational attainment at a faster rate than the Russians.

As indigenous populations became better educated, moved to the cities, and gained more representation in prestigious professions, they increasingly came into competition and conflict with Russians. A certain amount of assimilation to the dominant Russo-Soviet culture did take place, and national groups were in a much weaker position if they occupied lower-level territorial units such as autonomous republics rather than union republics. In general, however, over the postwar decades Russification was strong enough to antagonize the non-Russian nationalities but not strong enough to weaken national sentiment.

As in other multi-ethnic states, language use was among the most emotionally and politically charged issues. It was one of the blank spots in the indigenization that resumed in the 1950s. According to a controversial language reform of 1958-9, parents were to have the right to exercise choice about the language in which their children were educated. While this might sound like an enlightened multicultural measure, in many parts of the Soviet Union it was interpreted – correctly – as a means of Russification: in practice, non-Russian parents would choose to have their children educated in Russian, not the other way around.

In certain parts of the union, accordingly, Russians' knowledge of the local language was lamentable. In Central Asia and in the Azerbaijan republic, well under 10% of the local Russian population could be considered fluent in the local language. In the 1970 census, the first to contain such data, only 3% of Russians stated that they were fluent in another Soviet language (and in most cases that language was Ukrainian, a Slavonic language closely related to Russian). Conversely, linguistic Russification of the education system for non-Russians was strengthened in the

1970s and 1980s. By the early 1970s, the Belorussian capital Minsk had no schools in which the language of instruction was Belorussian. Russian remained the language of upward mobility in the Soviet Union, and non-Russians had every incentive to learn it. Demographic factors also tended towards Russification: increased rates of intermarriage between nationalities (especially given the shortage of men following World War II) often led to the adoption of Russian nationality by the children. Further waves of eastward Russian migration to new agricultural projects and construction sites in Kazakhstan and Siberia spread Russian influence still further.

Yet, considering all the factors in favour of the Russian language, linguistic Russification made strikingly little headway in the postwar decades. Its main successes occurred, as one might expect, in the westernmost Slavic republics of Ukraine, Belorussia, and the Russian Republic itself (whose autonomous republics offered relatively little support for indigenous languages and cultures). But other union republics – especially Estonia and Armenia, but also Azerbaijan, Georgia, Tajikistan, and Turkmenistan – experienced little Russification. Some even 'de-Russified'. Between 1959 and 1989, the proportion of non-Russians claiming Russian as their first language rose from just under 11% to just over 13%. Most of this change, moreover, took place between 1959 and 1979: by the 1980s, it had slowed down markedly.

Even the prime institution of patriotic integration – the army – did rather little to override national distinctions. Although the sole language of command was Russian, ethnic groups tended to hang together. And the army itself did much to encourage this ethnic identification: non-Slavs had only limited upward mobility, and were much less likely than Russians or Ukrainians to be assigned to combat units. The effect of military service for many Central Asians seems to have been to give them a much keener sense of their own ethnicity.

Not only did the non-Russians largely fail to adopt a Russified Soviet identity, they also had raised expectations of what the Soviet state could give them. The new generation of educated professionals that was trained up in the Caucasus and Central Asia in the 1950s and 1960s met frustrations in the 1970s, as the economically stagnant Soviet system could not provide them with an adequate supply of rewarding and prestigious employment. The high birth rates in the southern republics exacerbated the problem by increasing the number of indigenous school and university graduates. Upward mobility for local elites slowed markedly at the end of the 1960s.

But the opportunities of the previous two decades had already put in place a far more 'indigenized' elite that was increasingly ready to treat its home republic as a homeland and a patrimony. Party leaders in the republics might now acquiesce in, or even encourage, demonstrations of national feeling. In 1959, the party elites in Latvia and Azerbaijan were purged for failing to comply with the new language legislation. In 1966, the first party secretary in Armenia lost his job for failing to prevent demonstrations to mark the 50th anniversary of the Armenian genocide by the Turks. In 1972, the Ukrainian and Georgian party bosses were removed for nationalism. In 1978, all the same, several thousand Georgians took to the streets to protest against Moscow's attempt to tamper with the newly declared status of Georgian as the state language of their republic.

As always, regional representatives of the Soviet system had to be adept at squeezing resources from the centre. But the usual lobbying for resources now took on a more national colouring. It also sometimes shaded into outright corruption. In 1959, the Uzbek party boss was revealed to have spent 7 million rubles on building a dacha; he had evidently outgrown his previous house, though this had a swimming pool and was situated on an estate of 27 hectares.

The unravelling of Soviet federalism

For all their dabbling in nationalism, party functionaries in the 1960s and 1970s remained loyal to the system that fed them. But this period also saw the rise of various forms of nationalist self-assertion at the grass roots. The most extreme cases came in the Baltic states and western Ukraine, which had waged partisan war against the Soviet authorities in the late 1940s. Even in the 1960s, Ukrainians accounted for perhaps half of the political prisoners in the Soviet Union, and in Estonia the last surviving member of the postwar Baltic partisans, the Forest Brothers, was tracked down by the KGB only in 1978. Though cases of open opposition were now rare, in the post-Stalin era nationalist sentiment in Ukraine and the Baltics found less militant expression in the human rights movement and in forms of cultural revival such as folklore and religion. Khrushchev's denunciation of Stalin was followed by a revival of local nationalism in Georgia and Armenia. From the late 1960s onwards, two Soviet 'nationalities' – Germans and Jews – began to depart for newly accessible homelands in the Federal Republic of Germany and Israel. Between 1971 and 1979, more than a quarter of a million Jews left the USSR. More generally, the 1970s saw increasing cultural conflict over issues such as language use, religious freedom, workplace discrimination, resource distribution, and the right of particular nationalities to return from places of political exile.

The stirrings of nationalist revival were also felt in Russia, the one part of the Soviet Union that might be thought not to have needed it. After all, ethnic Russians were greatly overrepresented in party and state structures, and Soviet civilization was firmly under the sway of a Russian cultural pantheon and a Russian-dominated cult of World War II. But Russians could claim to have been victims of the Soviet experience no less than any other ethnic group – collectivization and terror had hit them very hard – and even the relatively benign aspects of Soviet modernization might serve to heighten their national consciousness. Mass urbanization, the depopulation of rural areas, and the slight liberalization of public expression in the 1950s made possible forms of cultural revival that would have been unthinkable under Stalin. A section of the literary intelligentsia began to write lyrically of the fast-disappearing world of the Russian village, and the 1960s saw the birth of a Russian heritage movement. Here was the closest Soviet Russia would come to a civil society before the Gorbachev period.

But Russian nationalism was not just a matter of cultural renaissance. It also fed off xenophobia and resentment. As indigenization once more gained force in the later Soviet period, many Russians became convinced that they were giving more to the socialist union than they were receiving from their fellow republics. This view was increasingly shared by a more nationalistic party elite in the RSFSR and by a section of the literary elite whose zeal for Russian culture was too often accompanied by hostility to other ethnic groups (above all Jews).

By the 1980s, then, the multinational community of the Soviet Union was a distinctly fractious place. But rising national sentiment, though it was a powerful catalyst for the unravelling of the Soviet system, cannot be seen as the prime cause. What changed in the mid-1980s was not the behaviour of national elites, and still less the behaviour of peoples, but rather that of the leadership in Moscow. If the regional leaders of the 1960s and 1970s were adept at squeezing resources out of the centre without ever questioning the system on which their well-being depended, those of the late 1980s had to operate in a much more risky environment where the centre was changing the rules of the game. In this context, a more assertive autonomist nationalism might prove to be the best bet.

National issues became a very public matter after Mikhail Gorbachev launched his policy of *glasnost* (openness). They gained a new political edge in the summer of 1987, when the Crimean

Tatars (deported *en masse* in May 1944) conducted an unprecedented demonstration in Moscow for the right to return to their homeland from Uzbekistan. The ensuing opportunities for civic action were seized most impressively in the Baltic states, where popular fronts gave democratization a national colouring and newly democratized supreme soviets took up the cause of national liberation from the Soviet ethno-federal state. In March 1990, the parliament in Lithuania – the most assertive and least ethnically Russian of the Baltic republics – voted to restore the independence that had been violated by the Soviet invasion of 1940; within weeks, Estonia and Latvia had followed suit.

The Baltics were a striking, but also a special, case. In Estonia, Latvia, and Lithuania, nationalism had a clarity of purpose that was lacking elsewhere: the cause was the re-establishment of independent nations that had been swallowed up by the Soviet Union during World War II. The lines were drawn clearly between separatist political movements and the 'centre' in Moscow. Although this stand-off led to bloodshed in January 1991, when Soviet security forces attempted to restore the status quo in the Lithuanian capital Vilnius, the independence movement retained its momentum.

In other places, however, decades or centuries of migration and intermarriage, along with the sometimes arbitrary Soviet drawing of territorial boundaries, meant that disengagement from the union would be a painful affair where the main opposition was not between centre and regions but between different regions. The most violent example in the late 1980s came in the autonomous region of Nagorny Karabakh, which since 1921 had existed as a primarily Armenian enclave embedded in the hostile neighbouring republic of Azerbaijan. The imposition of Soviet power in the South Caucasus in 1920 brought an end to armed conflict between Armenians and Azeris, but the weakening of central power in the 1980s emboldened Armenian deputies in Karabakh to demand the unification of their region with Armenia. What followed was a rapid slide from violent skirmishes to mass population displacement and war; a ceasefire came only in 1994.

The Karabakh situation showed a very different dynamic from that of the Baltic states. If Estonia, Latvia, and Lithuania were seeking liberation from the Soviet-Russian yoke, Armenia and Azerbaijan were more hostile to each other than to the Russians (Georgia, the third republic in the South Caucasus, was closer to the Baltic pattern, since its relations with the Soviet state had taken an antagonistic turn with the repression of patriotic pro-Stalin protest in 1956). The case of the Central Asian republics also undermines easy interpretations of the Soviet collapse as national liberation or de-imperialization. Speculation on the Islamic threat to the Soviet state proved to be greatly exaggerated. To the extent that there was conflict and violence, it resulted more often from economic grievances and local ethnic tensions than from broader national self-assertion. The worst violence in Central Asia at the end of the Soviet period – riots near the Kyrgyz city of Osh in June 1990 which killed more than 200 – was caused not by anti-Russian sentiment but by the resentment of impoverished Kyrgyz towards the rich Uzbeks who dominated the local economy. Nor were Central Asian political leaders necessarily hostile to Moscow. More often than not – and especially in Kazakhstan and Turkmenistan – power remained in the hands of communist-era elites who acted carefully and pragmatically as they disengaged themselves from Soviet political and economic structures.

The relationship between Soviet 'centre' and national 'periphery' was all the more tangled in the primarily Slavic parts of the USSR. Of all the republics, Ukraine perhaps best exemplified the problems and successes of the Soviet national balancing act. Here was a potential nation split down the middle between a Ukrainian-speaking western half and a Sovietized Russian-speaking eastern half. The gap between the two was unbridgeable, which might seem to have made strife and state breakdown a strong possibility. The first democratic elections in Ukraine, of March 1990, only confirmed regional differences. But, precisely because divisions between west and east were such an inescapable fact, some local communists began selectively to adopt Ukrainian nationalism as a way of maintaining the territorial unity that guaranteed their power. The collapse of Soviet institutions in Moscow after the failed communist coup of 19–21 August 1991 removed all equivocations: three days later the Ukrainian parliament voted for independence by 346 to 1. Ukrainian independence – like the dissolution of the Soviet Union that followed in December 1991 – was not a cause pushed through by popular protest. Rather, it was a measure taken with minimal discussion by a political elite under the pressure of events and only later ratified by a popular vote (a referendum of early December 1991 delivered an overwhelming majority in favour of independence). With the exception of the Baltic states, the last winter of the Soviet system had not been a springtime of peoples.

But the most ambiguous successor nation to the Soviet Union was Russia itself. The Russians had so automatically associated themselves with the USSR, and were so dependent on the great power identity that this country provided, that their place in a dismembered union was not altogether clear. Was Russia simply what would remain after the departure of all the recalcitrant republics from the USSR? How could it lay claim to any cultural or ethnic coherence when its own population was so mixed, and when so many 'Russians' remained in the former Soviet republics of the 'near abroad'? How could it build up national institutions to replace those of the Soviet Union? These were awkward questions for Russian politicians in the late 1980s and early 1990s. Some public figures were unambiguously committed to maintaining the USSR. Others overlooked or fudged the growing contradiction between Soviet institutions (headed by Gorbachev) and the emerging Russian institutions (headed by Boris Yeltsin, who was elected Russia's first president in June 1991). Still others – notably Yeltsin himself – seized the moment to throw off the carapace of the Soviet Union and set up a new Russian state with a liberal, non-ethnic, definition of citizenship.

When Russia began to shake itself free of the USSR, the Soviet state truly was doomed. But even the break-up of the union demonstrated a central paradox of the Soviet ethno-national experiment: this state, which in the 1930s and 1940s had been responsible for appalling campaigns of violence against various ethnic groups, had been a maker, not a breaker, of nations. The Bolsheviks had come to power in an empire where class and nationality were completely intertwined; their political descendants lost power in a state where the bankruptcy of Bolshevik class labels, and the processes of social and cultural modernization over which the Soviet Union had presided, made national allegiances far more meaningful than class. Soviet people were acutely aware of ethnic difference and reluctant to trade it for a purely civic notion of nationality. When the government of the now independent Russian Federation attempted in the mid-1990s to abandon the compulsory ethnic designation of the infamous 'fifth paragraph' in internal passports, this impeccably liberal measure met strong opposition from minority groups (Tatars and Bashkirs especially) who did not want to lose this Soviet administrative hook on which to hang their ethnicity. The law of unintended consequences has rarely been so richly illustrated as by the history of Soviet nationalities.

Chapter 6
West and East

'Russia and the West' is one of the perennial themes of Russian cultural and intellectual history. In the 20th century it became politically charged as never before. A line was drawn between the progressive Soviet state and the rapacious, untrustworthy, bourgeois powers that were waiting to pounce if it stumbled on its historical path. In the Stalin period, 'servility to the West' was consistently among the most heinous of political crimes.

The international hinterland of Bolshevism

It would be easy to conclude that Soviet self-understanding prescribed simple antipathy to 'the West'. But a closer look at the imagined geography of Soviet socialism reveals a more nuanced picture. One obvious complicating circumstance is the fact that many of the men who led the Bolshevik revolution had spent their maturity in Western Europe. Between 1900 and April 1917, Lenin led a peripatetic existence in Switzerland, Austria-Hungary, Germany, Britain, and elsewhere, returning to Russia only in an unsuccessful bid to shake up the revolutionary politics of 1905–7. The Bolsheviks' opponents would conclude from such prolonged absences that they were at best out of touch with Russian realities and at worst agents of Western governments bent on destabilizing the Russian empire. However, while Lenin opposed the war, wished passionately for tsarist Russia's defeat, and was willing to take whatever help he could get from the Germans to that end, he was no bourgeois stooge.

A safer conclusion to draw from the European pedigree of the leading Bolsheviks was that these men were deeply preoccupied with the parallels and interrelations between Russian and wider European developments. One key question they rarely stopped asking was the extent to which Russia would follow the model of revolution extrapolated by Marx from Western European developments.

The other matter of pressing concern was the extent to which revolutions in Russia and the West could be simultaneous and mutually reinforcing. As World War I continued into its third year, there were increasing reasons to believe that the material exhaustion of the combatants and the moral bankruptcy of their causes would make possible pan-European revolution. Back in 1914, Lenin had been appalled as European socialist parties had backed the war efforts of their respective national governments. Now, however, conditions were favourable for the overthrow of the bourgeois order. War and international affairs were crucial to Lenin's telescoping of the revolution from two stages into one. Leon Trotsky, the first People's Commissar for Foreign Affairs, reputedly declared that all he would need to do in his new role was 'issue a few revolutionary proclamations and then shut up shop'.

Before long, however, international ambitions had to be scaled down in the interests of preserving the socialist state. The first task of Bolshevik foreign affairs was a thankless one: to extricate Russia from a world war that it was in no position to fight. In March 1918, at Brest-Litovsk, Soviet Russia signed a peace treaty with Germany that was deeply controversial within the party. Fighting off opposition from advocates of 'revolutionary war', in early 1918 Lenin opposed the 'blind gamble' of fighting on against the Germans in the hope that revolution would soon break out in the West. The desperate condition of the Russian army, and the unwillingness of peasant soldiers to fight revolutionary war, were further arguments in favour of even a crudely 'annexationist' peace. No matter that the terms offered by the Germans would shrink the western part of the Russian state to 16th-century dimensions, deprive the former Russian empire of most of its iron ore and coal, and reduce its population by 56 million. The Soviet state now had incalculable importance as the flagship of world socialism, and that role must not be jeopardized. From this moment onwards, the ideological commitment to international revolution had to be tempered by the pragmatic need to keep socialism alive.

Russia's erstwhile allies in the war against Germany were horrified at this separate peace. Since the February Revolution they had sought to back forces in Russia that pledged to continue the war effort. After the Brest-Litovsk treaty they could entertain no illusions about the Bolshevik contribution to the war, and in due course landed troops in northern Russia and Siberia as well as lending support to various anti-Bolshevik causes in the civil war. Yet, although allied intervention in 1918–20 left an enduring legacy of resentment and suspicion, its impact was not decisive: the British and French were too preoccupied elsewhere, too militarily exhausted after four years of war, and too divided in their aims to bring the Bolsheviks down.

As for the international revolution, there were reasons for Bolshevik hopes to revive in late 1918 and early 1919. The end of World War I brought social crisis in the defeated states of East-Central Europe. Hungary had a communist government between March and August 1919. Several major cities in Germany were gripped by revolution from early November 1918, and Munich even saw a short-lived 'soviet republic' in April 1919. In due course, however, it became clear that Bolshevik-style revolution would not take place in Germany: the local communists were far weaker than the well-established indigenous socialists, who had plenty to hope for from democratic politics and no incentive to stake everything on insurrection. A new 'Weimar' constitution, signed in August 1919, brought the revolutionary era to a symbolic close.

Nonetheless, in March 1919 the cause of international revolution gained an organizational home with the creation of the Communist International (Comintern), which pledged to fight for the overthrow of the world's bourgeoisie and the triumph of international socialism. By the second Comintern congress, held in Moscow in July–August 1920, Bolshevik Russia had established centralized leadership and strict ideological control of the organization.

Whether it was worth aspiring to the leadership of the international communist movement was another matter. Admittedly, the prospects for European revolution briefly revived in 1920. Poland turned down the territorial settlement proposed by the Soviet government and sent its army deep into Ukraine with the support of Ukrainian nationalist troops. By June, however, the Red Army was driving the Poles back, and by August it was within reach of Warsaw. At this point, however, the Poles counter-attacked and the Soviets were routed. An armistice followed in October, and with it disappeared the last chances of spreading communism west.

Since Bolshevik long-term strategy had been predicated on the collapse of world capitalism, readjustment was required. A proletarian internationalist party had come to power only to find divisions between its own state and other nations entrenched as never before. How was a balance to be struck between Soviet national interests and the long-term cause of world revolution?

The solution was a pragmatic approach that was formulated in the mid-1920s by the slogan 'socialism in one country'. For the medium term, Soviet Russia would have to secure its position in a hostile international environment. The scarring experience of foreign intervention during the civil war in Siberia, Murmansk and Arkhangelsk, and the south was still vivid in the Bolshevik mind. The period 1917–20 had seen non-stop diplomatic conflict. The first

Soviet representative in London, Maxim Litvinov, had been arrested and held hostage by the British in 1918. In 1919, Bolshevik Russia had laboured in almost total diplomatic isolation. In the early 1920s, however, there was no alternative to manoeuvring within the postwar status quo. Finding itself in a weak and beleaguered position, the Soviet state had to mount a diplomatic rearguard action.

The Genoa Conference of April–May 1922 seemed propitious. This meeting was planned as an opportunity to soothe postwar resentments and establish a basis for cooperation in Europe. As an attempt to settle the relationship between Soviet Russia and the Western allies, however, it foundered on the issue of Russia's financial obligations to its creditors. In 1924, Soviet Russia did achieve formal recognition by Britain, France, and Italy. But progress remained limited on economic issues – especially the credits that Russia desperately needed. As early as March 1918, Lenin had identified the urgent need to catch up technologically so as to avoid future beatings at the hands of the capitalist powers. His judgement was that the logic of capitalism would compel the West to shelve its ideological proclivities and invest in Russia. The reality of the 1920s was rather different.

Soviet Russia did, however, find economic succour from an unlikely source. An undesirable (from the Franco-British point of view) consequence of the Genoa Conference was that Germany and Russia struck a deal with each other. According to the Treaty of Rapallo, signed in April 1922, the two pariah nations of postwar Europe cancelled all claims against each other, re-established full diplomatic relations, and agreed to far-reaching and mutually beneficial economic contacts. In Western Europe, 'Rapallo' would serve as shorthand for Russo-German conspiracy. Germany would remain Soviet Russia's most significant economic partner until World War II.

The case of Germany exemplified Bolshevik pragmatism. International relations had to be tactical, and perhaps the most promising tactic of all was to play the capitalist powers off against each other. But even in the 1920s, there were discomforting signs that these powers might themselves cooperate against the Soviet Union, and the Bolsheviks never shed their basic assumption that the West was inherently hostile to the Soviet order. The mid-1920s saw worrying signs of a rapprochement between Germany and the Western powers that would call into question the Rapallo agreement: the Dawes Plan of 1924 agreed terms for German reparation payments, and the Locarno treaties of October 1925 secured the western frontiers of Germany (though not, to Soviet concern, those in the east). In 1927 came a series of diplomatic disasters: the violent repression of the Chinese communist party, the severance by Britain of relations with the USSR, the assassination of the Soviet representative in Warsaw, and the failure of economic negotiations with France. When elaborated on the pages of *Pravda* and in the speeches of leading Bolsheviks, these events triggered a war scare that lodged firmly the theme of Western perfidy in Soviet public discourse. In a menacing precedent, the charge of naïve internationalism was used by Stalin and his allies as a tactic against their rivals in the party.

Thus, while the Soviet Union needed foreign assistance to aid its economic and military recovery, its relations with Western states were becoming inflammatory towards the end of the 1920s. To an extent, the existence of Comintern allowed the USSR to pursue a two-track foreign policy, striking convenient deals with capitalist powers while giving vent to its internationalist anti-capitalist militancy. But the Western powers were hardly fooled, and Soviet objectives were themselves confused. Economic self-interest, ideology, and geopolitics were frequently in tension or contradiction. On the one hand, the Depression was good from a Soviet point of view, as it threw world capitalism into crisis; on the other hand, it was thoroughly bad, as it greatly reduced the amount of economic aid the Soviet Union could expect to receive as it launched its crash industrialization programme. Or, to take another example, the Soviets encouraged German resentment at the postwar Versailles settlement as a way of finding themselves an ally in a hostile Europe, but by doing so they also made international conflict more likely and in the long run undermined the security of the USSR. By anathematizing European socialism as 'social fascism', moreover, the Comintern played its part in the rise of Nazism.

Western borrowings

But the skulduggery of international politics did not necessarily mean that the Bolsheviks were hostile to all things foreign. 'Culturedness' in the 1920s was very often near-synonymous with good 'Western' attributes such as personal hygiene, good time-keeping, and technical expertise. In 1923, Trotsky observed that: 'Through the revolution, our people opened a window onto Europe for themselves – by "Europe" we mean culture – just as, over two hundred years ago, the Russia of Peter the Great opened not a window, but a peephole onto Europe for the elite of the aristocratic-bureaucratic system.' But in his view they still had some way to go. With a few exceptions, Russian workers lacked 'the most elementary habits and notions of culture (in regard to tidiness, instruction, punctuality, etc.)' – attributes that their Western European counterparts could take for granted.

In this early phase of Soviet history, America most often played the role of the 'Good West' (as opposed to the 'Bad Old West' of, notably, Britain). America might be brazenly capitalist, but it was not (to the Soviet way of thinking) 'imperialist', it was not held back by the iniquitous political traditions of the 'old' world, and it shared with Russia the destiny of settling and developing enormous expanses of territory. While Soviet depictions of the USA regularly drew attention to poverty and racism as indictments of capitalism, they also dwelled admiringly on American technological expertise, organizational know-how, and work ethic. America was practically synonymous with modernity for Soviet people in the 1920s. Henry Ford and Frederick Taylor (the prophet of 'scientific' management techniques) were among the greatest heroes of the age. As late as December 1931, Stalin was willing to profess in public his admiration for 'the efficiency that the Americans display in everything – in industry, in technology, in literature and in life'.

On a diplomatic level, Soviet–American relations remained frosty: the Republican administrations of the 1920s refused to recognize the socialist state, and it took the Depression to bring this about (in 1933). But Soviet–American contacts of a non-governmental kind were intense between 1922 and 1931. In the summer of 1922, the American Relief Administration fed 11 million Soviet citizens each day, preventing the famine from assuming even more calamitous proportions. By the second half of the decade, dozens of Americans were helping to run farms in southern Russia, and tens of thousands of American tractors were assisting Soviet agriculture.

Soviet appreciation for American know-how was most pronounced in the all-important sphere of industrial technology. In the late 1920s, General Electric signed up to a vast programme of technical assistance to the Soviet Union. An American firm acted as consultants on the Dneprostroi project to build a gigantic hydroelectric dam on the Dniepr river in Soviet Ukraine. About 90% of the equipment for the Stalingrad Tractor Factory was bought in America, and by 1931 Stalingrad was home to the largest group of American workers anywhere in the Soviet Union (almost 400). Americans were heavily involved in other signature projects of the first five-year plan such as the Magnitogorsk steel mill. According to US government figures, Soviet purchases of American industrial equipment rose by a factor of four between 1927–8 and 1929–30. They finally began to flatten out in 1932, when the Depression was lowering prices for grain and reducing the Soviet capacity to pay for high technology imports. All told, the number of foreign engineers in the Soviet Union rose from almost none in 1924 to 9,000 (about a quarter of them American, most of the rest German).

On the technical front, the Americans were highly influential but always outdone in quantitative terms by the cheaper and more available Germans. American influence was perhaps at its greatest in the cultural sphere. By the mid-1920s, the USA was the unquestioned champion of the popular culture industry – especially cinema, an impeccably mass medium of great interest to the Bolsheviks. In 1925, 87% of films shown in the Soviet Union were foreign. Stars such as Douglas Fairbanks, Mary Pickford, Charlie Chaplin, Buster Keaton, and Harold Lloyd attained phenomenal popularity. In 1924, the Soviets set up a new state cinema company, Sovkino, to reduce the dependence on imported mass culture. But Soviet directors, if they were to succeed with audiences, could not diverge too far from Western formulas and motifs. 'American' plot design (cliffhangers), genres (melodrama), and even characters were abundant in the output of the 1920s. In *The Extraordinary Adventures of Mr West in the Land of the Bolsheviks* (directed by Lev Kuleshov in 1924), a YMCA president visits Moscow and brings along a Wild West cowboy as a bodyguard. Their acute suspicion of all things Bolshevik does not prevent them becoming easy prey for the NEP demi-monde.

17. **Mr West flies the flag in the land of the Bolsheviks**

The emergence of Soviet chauvinism

From 1927 onwards, however, Bolshevik toleration of foreign cultural influence tailed off steeply. During the period of cultural revolution, the number of foreign films shown in the Soviet Union declined from 68 in 1929 to 43 in 1930 to nought in 1932. Thereafter, numbers climbed back to a low ceiling of about 10 per year for the rest of the 1930s. Practitioners of the other arts were regularly reprimanded for 'formalism' – in other words, for showing unhealthy signs of decadent modernism. A prominent victim of this anti-Western puritanism was the outstanding young composer Dmitry Shostakovich, whose opera *Lady Macbeth of the Mtsensk District* was suddenly denounced at the end of January 1936.

Cultural policy was but one symptom of an isolationist and xenophobic turn in Soviet thinking. Stalin first used the slogan of 'socialism in one country' in December 1924, and by the 15th Party Congress in December 1927 he was moved to assert that 'the period of "peaceful coexistence" is receding into the past, giving place to a period of imperialist assaults and preparation for intervention against the USSR'. The reliance on Western expertise for the Great Leap Forward was increasingly contradicted by suspicion of capitalist 'wreckers' and of all Soviet people who had had dealings with them. Foreign contacts – even in the past – would have fatal consequences for many leading Bolsheviks in the show trials of the 1930s. The Soviet Union would take Western assistance as it sought to overcome its backwardness, but the West was always seen as predatory.

There were good reasons for Soviet foreign policy to become more bullish in the early 1930s: the Depression seemed to indicate conclusively that the implosion of world capitalism was not far off and raised the prestige (though not the material well-being) of Soviet socialism. But, as the 1930s wore on, tactical considerations continued to trump ideology. The Soviets were happy to see the West weak and divided, and to that end were happy to see a fall in support for the German socialist party (underestimating, like others, the Nazi threat). The prime concern was to defer war until a moment when the Soviet Union would be ready for it. To that end, the USSR joined the League of Nations in 1934. In 1935, Anthony Eden paid an official visit to the Kremlin; 'God Save the King' was played at the reception by order of Stalin. At the same time, the 'anti-fascist' cause could be promoted through the Soviet-dominated Comintern and in specific areas of foreign policy. The Spanish Civil War presented itself to the Soviet regime first as a huge propaganda coup and then as an opportunity to influence events in the far west of Europe on advantageous economic terms. Within three months of the outbreak of hostilities in July 1936, the USSR began to provide substantial military aid (for which it was well paid in Spanish gold), then scaling back its involvement in autumn 1937 when it was in its interests to do so.

The Munich agreement of September 1938, whereby Britain acquiesced in the German annexation of Czechoslovakia, forced yet another radical readjustment. The evidence was clear: the collective security policy had failed, and the Soviets could expect nothing but treachery from the imperialist British. When Hitler softened his rhetoric on Bolshevism, Stalin moved towards an agreement with Nazi Germany. The result was the Molotov–Ribbentrop pact of August 1939, whose secret protocols divided up East-Central Europe between Germany and Russia.

Stalin's intentions were to delay the war that he regarded as inevitable in the long term. But his calculations were based on an overestimate of the time it would take the Germans to overcome France and an underestimate of Hitler's willingness to take risks. In June 1941, the Germans invaded, and the Soviet regime once again had to take friends where it could find them. The result was the unlikely triumvirate of Stalin, Churchill, and Roosevelt. As a gesture of goodwill to his capitalist allies, Stalin was even willing to disband Comintern in 1943.

The Soviet Union

Map 2. The USSR and Europe at the end of World War II

18. A satirical cartoon from 1948. The mask of Ernest
Bevin slips to reveal the anti-Bolshevik Winston Churchill. The motif
of unmasking enemies was common in Stalin-era propaganda

The wartime alliance was at its strongest before the defeat of Germany was certain. From late 1943 onwards, as the issue of the postwar settlement loomed larger, irreconcilable differences came into view. The most intractable issue was Germany: neither side could agree to the country's reunification on the other's terms. Nor was there any prospect of Stalin relinquishing his idea of Eastern Europe as a strategic buffer zone. The ensuing Cold War was perhaps overdetermined given the number of geopolitical flashpoints and the ideological differences between the two superpowers. On the Soviet side, its causes lay in a paradoxical fusion of strength and weakness: the postwar the Soviet Union combined an enduring sense of vulnerability born of historical experience in the period 1914 to 1945 with an unprecedented capacity to exert geopolitical influence in locations from Vienna to Korea.

The early Cold War incited bursts of Soviet chauvinism. In 1947, marriages between Soviets and foreigners were forbidden. The attack on 'formalism' in the arts was renewed, with devastating consequences for the careers of several prominent writers and composers. In 1948, genetics was publicly excoriated as a 'bourgeois' science. A Lenin Prize was set up on the grounds that the Nobel Prize was clearly biased against the Soviets, who then occupied joint 13th–17th place in the medals table alongside Hungary, Tunisia, Spain, and India, but after Switzerland, Austria, and other 'second-rank' countries.

The ambiguities of the Cold War

Yet strange anomalies persisted. The taste for Western mass culture that was cultivated in the 1920s was once again indulged by foreign cinema. In his later years Stalin himself had a love of cowboy movies, which he viewed in his own cinema with his henchmen. An investigation in 1947 revealed that the USSR Society for Cultural Relations with Foreign Countries had obtained a copy of *Brief Encounter* from the British Embassy and had screened the film 15 times. For domestic production of cinema, this was a period of extreme dearth. Only 23 Soviet films were made in 1947, 13 in 1950, and 9 in 1951. Western cinema stepped into the breach. *Stagecoach* was renamed *The Journey Will Be Dangerous* and presented to the Soviet viewer as a story of Indian resistance to white colonization. Johnny Weissmuller, swimmer-turned-Tarzan, was the greatest film star of the age.

Postwar Russia even had its own Westernized youth subculture. Dubbed the *stilyagi*, its adherents adopted 'Tarzan haircuts', wore wide and colourful ties, and frequented a 'Cocktail Hall' on Moscow's main drag that had been set up in 1945 at a time of Soviet-American friendship and remained in existence through the early Cold War. While this subculture was a minority phenomenon – its origins lay in the gilded offspring of the Soviet functionaries who had at least some access to Western goods and cultural artefacts – it did serve notice that the fascination exerted by America on the Soviet public had not diminished since the 1920s.

The post-Stalin era saw continued lurching between repulsion and fascination in Soviet attitudes to the West. On the level of international relations, the Khrushchev period saw two-way diplomatic traffic that would have been unthinkable under Stalin. In 1955, Khrushchev broke through Cold War isolation and held talks with West German Chancellor Konrad Adenauer in Moscow. The Soviet leader kept up a frenetic travel schedule; his itinerary included summits in Geneva and Paris and state visits to Britain (where he met Queen Elizabeth) and the USA (where he met Marilyn Monroe). At the de-Stalinizing 20th Party Congress of February 1956, he brought peaceful coexistence back on the agenda: Soviet ideology no longer insisted that a new world war was inevitable. Yet Khrushchev also conducted himself brashly and belligerently in almost all the gatherings he attended, issued ultimatums that led to the construction of the Berlin Wall, and brought the superpowers the closest to nuclear war they would ever be when he recklessly raised the stakes in the Cuban Missile Crisis.

But Khrushchev's robust diplomacy was practised not only in the traditional geopolitical arena of the West. His many travels also took him to the decolonizing Third World. In October 1955, Khrushchev departed for a two-month trip to India, Burma, and Afghanistan where he tried to cultivate new ties following the collapse of colonialism. The Soviet Union saw itself as the natural friend of the 'non-aligned movement' of post-colonial nations. Over the next 30 years, it would entangle itself in the affairs (and the wars) of dozens of Third World states in locations from Angola to Vietnam.

The Soviet experience in the Third World reminds us that Marxism-Leninism did not only offer an abstract formula for Russia to catch up and overtake the West. Lenin had also provided what would be a highly influential set of theoretical models for analysing 'backward' societies – that is, societies that entered the early phase of industrial revolution with an enormous and undercapitalized rural sector, a weak bourgeoisie, and an autocracy untempered by constitutions. By the 1980s, Lenin was used to justify the policies of 27 regimes around the world with a total population of 1.25 billion. It is thus an oversimplification to dismiss Soviet socialism because it did not trigger proletarian revolution in Europe. Where it did make a big impact was in Asia and Africa. Lenin turned out to be a theorist of the Third World, not of the bourgeois West. And Soviet Russia could plausibly be seen as the vanguard of the developing world, not the bedraggled rear of the West.

The Soviet global mission was, however, compromised in two main ways. The first was that Third World 'clients' were often less than subservient to their enormous socialist patron. Time and again, from the 1960s to the 1980s, the Soviet Union funnelled arms and aid into regimes that – in Moscow's view – proved ungrateful and unworthy. Vast Soviet economic and military aid to Egypt in the

1960s did not prevent that country abruptly expelling Soviet military advisers in 1972 and allying with the Americans. By the mid-1970s, Iraq was the greatest Third World recipient of Soviet military aid, but it launched a terror campaign against its own communist party in 1978. In the 1960s and 1970s, the Soviet Union provided abundant aid to two neighbouring countries in East Africa, Somalia and Ethiopia, who then fought a war against each other. Worse still, the biggest and most powerful client of all – Maoist China – defiantly threw off Soviet tutelage, and by the late 1960s was seen by the Kremlin as at least as much of a geopolitical menace as the USA.

The other problem was that the Soviet leadership, whatever its rhetoric on the Third World, could not resist measuring itself by Western – above all, American – standards. Khrushchev was not averse to citing examples of US productivity to goad his own people into greater activity. As he told a meeting of state farm workers: 'if a capitalist farmer used eight kilos of grain to produce one kilo of meat, he'd have to go around without trousers. But around here a state farm director who behaves like that – his trousers are just fine.' Khrushchev's agricultural hero was the Iowa farming guru Roswell Garst, whom he invited to the USSR in the autumn of 1955. Khrushchev was an enthusiastic convert to maize, which he thought should be grown not only in fertile Ukraine but also in remote Yakutia and Chukotka.

But appreciative borrowing was the exception rather than the rule in Khrushchev's dealings with the Americans. He could rarely resist crude boasting. On arriving in the Oval Office, he thrust at President Eisenhower a replica of the Soviet rocket that had flown to the moon in autumn 1957. Sputnik – and then Gagarin's manned flight in 1961 – allowed Khrushchev to maintain that the Soviet Union had overtaken the advanced West in the fields of science and technology. On the agricultural front, admiration for the feats of Garst did not prevent Khrushchev promising that the USSR would shortly overtake the USA in per capita production of

West and East

meat, butter, and milk. On the cultural front, the Soviet Union was engaged in competition with the West in a wide range of fields: philosophy, literature, music, ballet, art, chess, and so on.

Although the Soviets might proclaim particular triumphs – if their man was first into space, or if their athletes scooped Olympic medals, or if their pianist won a major competition – this reflex to recognize the West as a benchmark had double-edged consequences. In the realm of popular culture, there was little doubt that America continued to lead the world. Propaganda for American values and the American way of life was dangerously effective. The media offensive from the West began in the first few years after the war, notably over the airwaves in the activity of Voice of America and Radio Liberation (later Liberty). In the 1950s, these stations shifted from naked ideological hostility to more subtle forms of influence: the approach was less to undermine the Soviet order directly than to show the virtues of the Western way. Although the Soviets started jamming Russian-language broadcasts in the late 1940s, there was little doubt that Western radio was attracting significant audiences all the way to the Urals. An unpublished survey by the Moscow city authorities in 1975 found that more than half of working people in the capital, and 80% of students, were listening to Western radio stations.

The post-Stalin era saw a substantial increase in contact between Soviet citizens and foreigners. From 1947 to 1951, American visitors to the Soviet Union numbered only a few dozen. In the second half of the 1950s, however, came a number of moves towards cultural cooperation, which, even if they thinly masked bitter competition at the state level, allowed Soviet people a much more extended peek at the West than they had ever been granted previously. One of the earlier and more extraordinary examples was the World Youth Festival held in Moscow in 1957. The Soviet capital threw its arms open to an unprecedented number of foreign visitors (including almost

19. A scene of revelry from the World Youth Festival, Moscow, 1957

1,000 foreign correspondents). The authorities attempted to rein in the festivities: strenuous efforts were made to ensure public order and decorum, and law-enforcement professionals were supplemented by 20,000 Komsomol members for the duration. Notwithstanding their efforts, urban folklore alleged the existence of a distinct cohort of 'festival children' born of mixed capitalist/socialist liaisons. In reality, the demographic effects of the festival were not nearly so drastic, but its cultural impact remained considerable.

The cultural agreements of the late 1950s also provided for an exchange of exhibitions: in the summer of 1959, the Soviets were given an Exhibition of Science, Technology, and Culture at the

New York Coliseum, while the Americans were allowed to put on a National Exhibition at Sokolniki Park in Moscow. Much as the Soviets might try to constrain the Americans in their preparations (by, for example, forbidding them from handing out free cosmetics to women or by organizing the heckling of the American guides), the exhibition made a stunning impression on the Soviet public. The official attendance figure was 2.7 million visitors over the six weeks of the exhibition; the daily figure was in excess of 60,000. The guides were bombarded with questions, most of them relating to the American standard of living. The 20 most-asked questions included: 'How much do American cigarettes cost?' and 'What is meant by the American dream?'

To an increasing (if still limited) extent, Soviet people were getting a piece of the wider world as well as merely admiring it from a distance. In 1956, 560,000 Soviet citizens went abroad, and about 1.5 million followed in the next two years. Even if most of these travellers were visiting the 'near West' of the Eastern European socialist bloc, they tended to find that the comparison was not in favour of the USSR. The Soviet education system was also permitting a more cosmopolitan world-view. By 1957, almost two-thirds of students in higher education were learning English, and in 1961 came an expansion of foreign-language tuition in secondary schools. Much contact with the West, however, came not through personal acquaintance or through formal institutions but through the media and consumer goods. The tape recorder (not to mention the radio) made possible the circulation of popular music. The craze for Western clothing went so far that the Soviet authorities for a while conducted negotiations with American firms for production of jeans under licence. Well-heeled Soviet youth adopted an Americanized slang to refer to the accessories necessary for a decent life: *shoozy* for the feet, a *voch* for the wrist, a *beg* over the shoulder – all accompanied by the requisite *leibel*.

Seventeen Moments of Spring

This series, Soviet television's greatest ever cult phenomenon, appeared in twelve 70-minute episodes in 1973. Adapted from a novel by the popular spy novelist Yulian Semyonov, its hero Max Otto von Stirlitz is a Soviet agent implanted in the Nazi elite. In February 1945, with Berlin under heavy bombardment, Stirlitz is entrusted with a crucial mission. The Soviet High Command has received information that someone at the very top of the Third Reich has made unofficial overtures to Allen Dulles with a view to concluding a separate peace at the expense of the USSR. Stirlitz has to find out who is behind the plan and then to foil it. While the basic conceit is fully in line with Cold War rhetoric – the implication is that the fascists and the capitalists are roughly equivalent in their hostility to Soviet Russia – its realization reveals a more ambivalent attitude to the West. Although Stirlitz is certainly a patriot – he permits himself an evening off on 23 February, the Day of the Red Army, to down vodka and roast potatoes in his fireplace – he is also so embedded in German society, and so affectionate towards the German people as a whole, that he occasionally forgets that he is not one of 'them'. Even the leading Nazis are not demonized but subtly characterized by well-known Soviet actors. And the series – shot in retro-style black-and-white with lingering close-ups – betrays more than a little fascination with the 'Western' way of life. Berlin may be under fire, but Stirlitz can still repair to his favourite watering hole, the café Elefant, and sip cognac. And at the end of a hard day, he can retreat to his well-appointed villa in a suburb apparently immune from bombing raids.

Gorbachev as Westernizer

Perhaps the most consequential aspect of Western influence was its role in forming the world-view of the politicians who would come to power in the 1980s. In January 1958, the Soviet and American governments set up an exchange programme for graduate students. The candidates chosen on the Soviet side were generally quite mature budding members of the elite. Aleksandr Yakovlev, later a member of Mikhail Gorbachev's inner circle, spent time at Columbia University in 1958–9. Oleg Kalugin, who later went from Soviet chief of counter-intelligence to active participant in the democratic politics of the perestroika era, was another member of the Columbia class of '58. As he recalled years after: 'I rode buses and subways for hours, and saw more than one hundred films. I went to a strip club in Greenwich Village, shelling out $40 for a drink with one of the dancers. I even won election to the Columbia University Student Council, undoubtedly the first KGB officer – and, I suppose, the last – to serve on that body.' While these experiences did not shake his belief in Soviet communism, he later spent a decade as a KGB officer in New York and Washington – which did change his world-view.

Mikhail Gorbachev himself was cosmopolitan by the unexacting standards of the Brezhnev era. In the 1970s, when still a regional party boss, he made tourist trips to Italy and France, and he also visited Belgium, Holland, and West Germany in an official capacity. In 1983, he headed a delegation to Canada, where he struck up a close relationship with the Soviet ambassador there, the Columbia alumnus Aleksandr Yakovlev. What Gorbachev saw on his travels – from Dutch social democracy to Canadian mechanized agriculture – contributed to a flexible and tolerant approach that was wholly unprecedented among Soviet leaders. As Gorbachev later recalled, during a summit on Malta in 1989 he got talking with President George Bush and Secretary of State James Baker on 'whether it is possible to talk about "Western values" as the basis for the new course of development in the world'. In Gorbachev's view, 'the main thing was the openness of different kinds of societies in relation to one another and not scholastic ideological disputes that threaten to become some sort of new "holy war" '. His interlocutors were happy to agree that 'democratic values' were the way forward.

This was a pleasant ecumenical vision of post-Cold War harmony, but the reality was that most people's ideological map of the world continued to feature a fault-line between East and West. And the 'West' with which Gorbachev negotiated the end of the Cold War was not Finland or Belgium but the America of Ronald Reagan and George Bush. In the next few years Russia would indulge to the full its fascination with all things American – from films and fast food to capitalist robber barons. The USA would receive more than its fair share of blame for Russia's national humiliation in the 1990s, even if the reality was that more and more Russians were learning English, travelling abroad, and partaking of globalized consumerism (at a low but rising level).

Did the West, then, 'win' the Cold War? No one can seriously doubt that the Soviet Union was a profoundly flawed political and economic system that had no hope of keeping economic pace with prosperous liberal capitalism. But Soviet nostalgists would have several grounds for special pleading. Russia had, after all, started from a low base in 1917. It had saved the world – and practically ruined itself – in 1941–5. Above all, by turning a backward and devastated country from historical laggard to modern power, the Soviet Union had blazed a trail that many fellow 'Easterners' would seek to follow, and that had left many impressionable Westerners gasping in the middle third of the 20th century.

As it performed these feats, the USSR always had an imagined West as its key point of reference: as bugbear, as bogeyman, sometimes as exemplar. After centuries of 'orientalism' (Western imaginings of the East), it turned 'occidentalism' into a powerful way of construing the modern world. The question of whether Soviet Russia was, at bottom, 'Western' or 'Eastern' is futile. The key point is that it did more than any other state to define what 'West' and 'East' might mean in the 20th century. Given that these terms seem unlikely to lose their currency anytime soon, this is no small legacy.

Conclusion

I suspect that all Russia-watchers of a certain age still feel from time to time a jolting sense of disorientation at the sudden disappearance of the country that enveloped much of Eurasia until so recently and that seemed so permanent and powerful to those who grew up in the 1980s, let alone the 1960s or 1940s. The widespread and prolonged adoption of the tag 'postcommunist' suggests that we have struggled to know what to do about the collapse of the USSR; it is as if we are waiting for the rubble of that gigantic country to lift and reveal a new set of historical signposts for Russia and the wider world. A meaningful parallel can be drawn between 1991 and 1917: historical interpretation of the Russian Revolution did not really gather momentum until 20 or 30 years after the fact, but then it did not let up for half a century. By that analogy, we can expect investigation of the Soviet experience to remain intense until 2050 or so. For those who have the stomach for it, there is much to look forward to.

The truism that each place and each era makes its own history is abundantly exemplified by the Soviet case. Western observers, even those relatively favourable to the Soviet Union, have often chosen to focus on phenomena a long way from the cultural mainstream of Soviet Russia – witness the fascination with the more outlandish manifestations of the early Soviet avant-garde or the preference for

Eisenstein's *Battleship Potemkin* over the Stalinist musicals whose box office appeal was vastly greater. In the last 30 years, Soviet studies have been swept by the global academic fashion for studying genuinely 'popular' culture; Stalinist movies and the like are now receiving their due. What lies ahead, presumably, is a more sustained engagement with later Soviet civilization – from Sputnik in 1957 to the Moscow Olympics of 1980.

Another source of fresh perspectives is periodization. As I suggested in the introduction to this book, the great majority of treatments of Soviet history, whether explicitly or implicitly, take the Revolution and the pre-war Stalin period as their point of reference: it is here that they look for the origins and the significance of the Soviet political, social, and cultural order. Perhaps, however, this approach understates the capacity for change of the Soviet 'system' and the wrenching impact of the Great Patriotic War. Between 1941 and 1945, the Soviet population was caught up in total war, suffered mass displacement and ethnic repression, took up a more active and empowered relationship to the state, and observed a far-reaching redefinition of the Soviet Union's position in the world. These are perhaps changes no less consequential than those of 1917–21.

My own approach has, in a sense, been to 'go native'. Soviet Russia had a notable predilection for binary oppositions: they pervaded official ideology in the form of the Marxist-Leninist dialectic, but they also had much currency in intellectual life even after Stalinist shackles loosened. In the 1960s and 1970s, a pioneering Soviet school of structuralism analysed the whole of human culture in terms of paired opposites, arguing along the way that Russian culture had a particular fondness for binaries. The pairs I have chosen for my chapter headings all had resonance in Soviet self-understanding, though they are by no means the only possibilities. Others might include 'men and women', 'city and village', and, not least, 'war and peace'. There are a hundred different ways to write a text as short as this on a subject as big as the Soviet Union. If readers come away from this book ready to think of a few of the other ninety-nine, then I will consider my job well done.

Rethinking the Soviet experience is still a worthwhile and exciting activity. Indeed, now that the USSR has 'historical interest only', it is all the more enticing to take an interest in it. The divisions between Russian and foreign research communities have (in principle, at least) lifted, and the Soviet Union is open to the same methods of investigation, and the interpretive frameworks, that have worked on other countries. Researchers can consult archives, conduct interviews, and travel freely. The Soviet Union can now – finally – escape the box marked 'area studies' and become part of world history. Here, perhaps, we have a belated fulfilment of the internationalism that was too often trumped by isolationism and xenophobia in the USSR's dealings with the outside world. In terms of intellectual insights, the Soviet Union has just as much to give the rest of the world as it stands to receive. It may have collapsed, but to say that it 'failed' is meaningless: complex societies and civilizations are not amenable to one-word assessments. One thing is certain: we have not the slightest chance of understanding the 20th century – or the early 21st – without giving the Soviet contribution to world history its due.

Further reading

General

There are several fine surveys of Soviet history that offer far more detail than this book. See, for example: Geoffrey Hosking, *A History of the Soviet Union 1917–1991* (1992); Ronald Grigor Suny, *The Soviet Experiment: Russia, the USSR, and the Successor States* (1998); and John Keep, *A History of the Soviet Union 1945–1991* (2nd edn., 2002).

Introduction

The histories of the Revolution discussed here are: Orlando Figes, *A People's Tragedy: The Russian Revolution, 1891–1924* (1996); Richard Pipes, *The Russian Revolution, 1899–1919* (1990) and *Russia under the Bolshevik Regime, 1919–1924* (1994); Sheila Fitzpatrick, *The Russian Revolution* (1982); S. A. Smith, *The Russian Revolution: A Very Short Introduction* (2002); Peter Holquist, *Making War, Forging Revolution: Russia's Continuum of Crisis, 1914–1921* (2002). A key work based on the Smolensk archive is Merle Fainsod, *Smolensk under Soviet Rule* (1958). For some of the findings of the Harvard Interview Project, see Raymond A. Bauer, Alex Inkeles, and Clyde Cluckhohn, *How the Soviet System Works: Cultural, Psychological, and Social Themes* (1956).

Chapter 1

On early Soviet visions of the future, see Richard Stites, *Revolutionary Dreams: Utopian Vision and Experimental Life in the Russian*

Revolution (1989). On the later cultural orthodoxy, see Régine Robin, *Socialist Realism: An Impossible Aesthetic* (1992). For various perspectives on the past in the Soviet Union, see Frederick C. Corney, *Telling October: Memory and the Making of the Bolshevik Revolution* (2004); Nina Tumarkin, *Lenin Lives! The Lenin Cult in Soviet Russia* (1983); and the same author's *The Living and the Dead: The Rise and Fall of the Cult of World War II in Soviet Russia* (1994).

Chapter 2

Important works on Soviet political violence include George Leggett, *The Cheka: Lenin's Political Police* (1981); J. Arch Getty and Oleg V. Naumov, *The Road to Terror: Stalin and the Self-Destruction of the Bolsheviks, 1932–1939* (1999); Lynne Viola et al. (eds.), *The War against the Peasantry, 1927–1930: The Tragedy of the Soviet Countryside* (2005); Jan T. Gross, *Revolution from Abroad: The Soviet Conquest of Poland's Western Ukraine and Western Belorussia* (2nd edn., 2002); Anne Applebaum, *Gulag: A History of the Soviet Camps* (2003). For various kinds of social and cultural context, see Stephen Kotkin, *Magnetic Mountain: Stalinism as a Civilization* (1995); Catriona Kelly, *Comrade Pavlik: The Rise and Fall of a Soviet Boy Hero* (2005); Karen Petrone, *Life Has Become More Joyous, Comrades! Celebrations in the Time of Stalin* (2000); Catherine Merridale, *Ivan's War: The Red Army 1939–45* (2005); Vladimir A. Kozlov, *Mass Uprisings in the USSR: Protest and Rebellion in the Post-Stalin Years* (2002).

Chapter 3

For various perspectives on Soviet economic life, see: Alec Nove, *An Economic History of the USSR, 1917–1991* (1992); Julie Hessler, *A Social History of Soviet Trade: Trade Policy, Retail Practices, and Consumption, 1917–1953* (2004); Jukka Gronow, *Caviar with Champagne: Common Luxury and the Ideals of the Good Life in Stalin's Russia* (2003); Elena Osokina, *Our Daily Bread: Socialist Distribution and the Art of Survival in Stalin's Russia, 1927–1941* (2001); Thane Gustafson, *Crisis among Plenty: The Politics of Soviet Energy under Brezhnev and Gorbachev* (1989).

Chapter 4

More on the topics covered in this chapter can be found in: T. H. Rigby, *Communist Party Membership in the USSR, 1917–1967* (1968); Sheila Fitzpatrick, *The Cultural Front: Power and Culture in Revolutionary Russia* (1992); Lewis H. Siegelbaum, *Stakhanovism and the Politics of Productivity in the USSR, 1935–1941* (1988); Vera S. Dunham, *In Stalin's Time: Middleclass Values in Soviet Fiction* (2nd edn., 1990); Basile Kerblay, *Modern Soviet Society* (1983).

Chapter 5

Important recent books on Soviet nationalities include: Jeremy Smith, *The Bolsheviks and the National Question, 1917–23* (1999); Terry Martin, *The Affirmative Action Empire: Nations and Nationalism in the Soviet Union, 1923–1939* (2001); Francine Hirsch, *Empire of Nations: Ethnographic Knowledge and the Making of the Soviet Union* (2005); Ronald Suny and Terry Martin (eds.), *A State of Nations: Empire and Nation-Making in the Age of Lenin and Stalin* (2001); Adrienne Edgar, *Tribal Nation: The Making of Soviet Turkmenistan* (2004). Old but good is Richard Pipes, *The Formation of the Soviet Union: Communism and Nationalism, 1917–1923* (2nd edn., 1964). On later Soviet nationality affairs, see Gerhard Simon, *Nationalism and Policy towards the Nationalities in the Soviet Union: From Totalitarian Dictatorship to Post-Stalinist Society* (1991). An invaluable work of reference is Robert J. Kaiser, *The Geography of Nationalism in Russia and the USSR* (1994).

Chapter 6

See, for example: Adam Ulam, *Expansion and Coexistence: The History of Soviet Foreign Policy, 1917–67* (1968); Denise J. Youngblood, *Movies for the Masses: Popular Cinema and Soviet Society in the 1920s* (1992); Leon Trotsky, *Problems of Everyday Life: Creating the Foundations for a New Society in Revolutionary Russia* (1973); William Taubman, *Khrushchev: The Man and His Era* (2003); David Caute, *The Dancer Defects: The Struggle for Cultural Supremacy during the Cold War* (2003).

Index

Index

Index

Expand your collection of
VERY SHORT INTRODUCTIONS

MODERN CHINA
A Very Short Introduction
Rana Mitter

China today is never out of the news: from human rights controversies and the continued legacy of Tiananmen Square, to global coverage of the Beijing Olympics, and the Chinese 'economic miracle'. It seems a country of contradictions: a peasant society with some of the world's most futuristic cities, heir to an ancient civilization that is still trying to find a modern identity. This *Very Short Introduction* offers the reader with no previous knowledge of China a variety of ways to understand the world's most populous nation, giving a short, integrated picture of modern Chinese society, culture, economy, politics and art.

'A brilliant essay.'

Timothy Garton, TLS

THE U.S CONGRESS
A Very Short Introduction
Donald Richie

The world's most powerful national legislature, the U. S.
Congress, remains hazy as an institution. This *Very Short
Introduction* to Congress highlights the rules, precedents, and
practices of the Senate and House of Representatives, and
offers glimpses into their committees and floor proceedings to
reveal the complex processes by which they enact legislation.
In *The U.S. Congress*, Donald A. Ritchie, a congressional
historian for more than thirty years, takes readers on a
fascinating, behind-the-scenes tour of Capitol Hill-pointing out
the key players, explaining their behaviour, and translating
parliamentary language into plain English.

SOCIAL MEDIA
Very Short Introduction

Join our community

www.oup.com/vsi

- Join us online at the official Very Short Introductions **Facebook** page.
- Access the thoughts and musings of our authors with our online **blog**.
- Sign up for our monthly **e-newsletter** to receive information on all new titles publishing that month.
- Browse the full range of Very Short Introductions online.
- Read **extracts** from the Introductions for free.
- Visit our library of **Reading Guides**. These guides, written by our expert authors will help you to question again, why you think what you think.
- If you are a teacher or lecturer you can order inspection copies quickly and simply via our website.